T0386125

Mortimer and the Witches

MORTIMER AND THE WITCHES

A History of Nineteenth-Century Fortune Tellers

Marie Carter

EMPIRE STATE EDITIONS

AN IMPRINT OF FORDHAM UNIVERSITY PRESS

NEW YORK 2024

Fordham University Press has no responsibility for the persistence or accuracy of URLs for external or third-party Internet websites referred to in this publication and does not guarantee that any content on such websites is, or will remain, accurate or appropriate.

Fordham University Press also publishes its books in a variety of electronic formats. Some content that appears in print may not be available in electronic books.

Visit us online at www.fordhampress.com.

Library of Congress Cataloging-in-Publication Data available online at https://catalog.loc .gov.

Printed in the United States of America

26 25 24   5 4 3 2 1

First edition

For Sarah Jensen
(1954–2022)

CONTENTS

Mortimer and the Witches

INTRODUCTION

Lenormand Card: Child (Meaning = *Innocence*)

Since 2015, I have worked as a tour guide educator and tour developer for Boroughs of the Dead, a walking tour company that specializes in macabre, strange, and ghostly histories of New York City. The seed of the idea for *Mortimer and the Witches* was planted over Halloween 2017. A pile of books with supernatural themes is a fixture by my bedside, and that night, while snuggled up in bed with my purring cat familiar, I pulled Susan Fair's *American Witches* from the stack.

When New York City began its life as a colony in the 1600s, its first settlers were Dutch. The Netherlands was the most liberal country in Europe, and the Dutch Calvinists did not share the same superstitions as the Pilgrims—spectral evidence, for example, was not admissible in the courts. Moreover, New Amsterdam was founded as a company town whose main purpose was to extract material goods from the colony for the Dutch West India Company. That meant New Amsterdam was exceptionally diverse. By the late 1640s, it was recorded that eighteen different languages were being spoken in the colony. The overarching attitude of the company town—except for some despot leaders—was that they didn't care where residents came from, what language they spoke, or what gods they worshipped. They cared more about the skills that could be placed in the service of the economy.

The only documentation of a witch trial in New York City[1] that I knew of is from 1665, shortly after the British seized New Amsterdam from the Dutch. That year, Ralph and Mary Hall of Setauket, Long Island

(Seatallcott back then), were accused of practicing witchcraft and poisoning their neighbor George Wood and the infant daughter of one Ann Rogers. The case went to trial in the Stadt Huys on October 2, 1665, and both Ralph and Mary Hall were acquitted, though Mary Hall was asked to appear at court three times just to prove she had been behaving herself.

I began reading Fair's *American Witches* under the assumption that there would be no mention of New York witches in this book and that all the stories would take place in New England, where the most famous witch trials occurred. So I was pleasantly surprised to encounter the chapter "Lifestyles of the Witch and Infamous: The Black Arts and Bad Neighborhoods of the Witches of New York," which described a book published in 1858 called *The Witches of New York*, written by someone with the wild, fantastical name Q. K. Philander Doesticks, P.B., the pseudonym of Mortimer Neal Thomson. Q. K. stood for "Queer Kritter," and P.B. stood for "Perfect Brick." The author appeared to be poking fun at pompous suffixes in his selection of "Perfect Brick"; "Brick" was once slang for a solid, reliable person.

After devouring Fair's hilarious—but all too brief—takedown of the Doesticks book, I was eager to read the original work. *The Witches of New York* was initially published as a series of articles for the *New-York Tribune* in 1857 before being published in book form. Perhaps as a way of lending his voice journalistic authority, Doesticks chose to write of himself in the third person, calling himself the "Cash Customer" and at other times going by the pseudonym of Johannes.

In a nutshell, Mr. Doesticks, P.B., had a twofold purpose in seeking to uncover the ridiculous and corrupt practices of fortune tellers in New York City. First, he wanted to prevent impressionable and innocent young ladies from taking up the dark arts of fortune telling because—the connection he makes is somewhat foggy—the practice was just one step away from prostitution. Second, he wanted to put a stop to naïve young women having their fortunes told by these crooked old hags. Doesticks was writing in the grand male tradition of preaching to women on how to conduct themselves properly, a genre all too prevalent during his lifetime. As Christine Stansell wrote in her book *City of Women*, "the belief in women's potential for deviousness is striking. Women's dependent status supposedly fostered in them all the vices and stratagems of the weak: They were foolish, easily corrupted by flattery, immodest and frivolous, artful and vain. And *because* they were so prone to these vices, they were rightfully and properly dependent on men for direction and moral authority."[2] More than just provide women with moral guidance, Doesticks also proposed to expose the absurd and woefully inaccurate predictions of these "witches," whom he labeled as such given their practice of the "black arts."

While the fortune tellers he wrote about appeared to be unreliable narrators, so was Doesticks. He would often provide false names, dates of birth, and other inaccurate information about himself. In one chapter, when he visited a rare male fortune teller, Dr. Wilson, the astrologist repeated the phrase, "If the time of birth given is correct. . . ." That is not something commonly said in an astrology reading, which suggests Dr. Wilson may have sensed something was off with his querent. Thomson wrote that his persona "Johannes drummed up his youthful recollections of that interesting event, and gave the day, the hour, and the minute, with his accustomed accuracy."[3] If Doesticks had been in character as Johannes during his visits, it is likely he created a fake time and place of birth, too.

Doesticks had also commenced his satirical polemic with an agenda in mind. His editor at the *Tribune*, Charles Anderson Dana, was reputed for chasing stories that would expose the scam artists and humbugs of the city. The premise of the Doesticks book was so rigid in its purpose that there was little room for viewing the (mostly) women that he visited through any other kind of lens.

Nonetheless, I was fascinated by my initial reading of the original Doesticks manuscript. Although I flinched a lot reading the misogynistic depictions of women, I did find his style entertaining and his descriptions of the neighborhoods he visited visceral and lively. One other beautiful aspect of this book from the perspective of a tour guide is that Doesticks provided all the original addresses for the fortune tellers, who mostly resided in poor areas of the Lower East Side. Most of them lived on *Broome* Street. Somehow Doesticks didn't pick up on the humor of visiting *witches* on Broome Street, but perhaps he was too focused on *whom* the street was named after, John Broome, a city alderman and the lieutenant governor of New York in 1804.

With *The Witches of New York* as a starting reference point, my boss Andrea Janes and I began developing a tour for Boroughs of the Dead. As I researched the tour and later conducted it, I became more curious about and empathetic toward the characters involved. To be sure, the predictions dispensed to Doesticks, if they were veraciously reported, do seem vague, inaccurate, and unhelpful. However, I couldn't help but feel sympathy for the struggles of these mostly working-class, immigrant women of the nineteenth century, and I felt their stories had more depth than Doesticks allowed. What other options did they have for making a reasonable income to support themselves and their family, if they had one?

What other professions offered women the kind of autonomy afforded by fortune telling? In my analysis and discussion of them, I wanted ultimately to look at them as three-dimensional figures rather than as the caricatures they had been reduced to in the original 1858 book.

Moreover, my own motivations and personal interest in visiting Tarot readers gave me pause in contemplating the purpose of those seeking out the advice of fortune tellers. Did querents believe absolutely everything they were told? Were they as naïve as Doesticks considered them? If not, would that then make the witches less nefarious than Doesticks's portrayal makes them out to be?

I was seventeen years old when I received my first Tarot reading, in Scotland, where I grew up. The Tarot reader was fundraising for a local dog rescue center where I was volunteering, and even though I did not believe anyone could predict the future, I was intrigued. The reader seemed to be confident in her powers of clairvoyance. I don't remember what she told me exactly, but I do remember thinking that nothing she said rang true. Nonetheless, I was fascinated by the process of fortune telling, and I began to wonder whether our desire to visit fortune tellers is deeper and more complex than merely the need for simple and accurate predictions of the future.

What left the most lasting impression on me was not any single prediction that I gleaned from that evening. It was the card deck my fortune teller used: the Shakespearean Tarot, which was gorgeously illustrated with various quotations from the plays. Each of the Major and Minor Arcana cards was represented by characters, scenes, and lines from Shakespeare. I later found out the deck was designed by Dolores Ashcroft-Nowicki, a British occult author whose grandmother was a full-blooded Romani. Ashcroft-Nowicki had studied at the Royal Academy of Dramatic Art in London. As an aspiring writer and lover of Shakespeare's works, I was fascinated by the art and quotations on the cards, and when I cross-referenced Tarot symbolism with the Shakespearean scenes depicted on the cards, I was astounded by the deck's complicated and thoughtful design. A friend had given me the Shakespearean Tarot deck for my eighteenth birthday, and I loved it so much it was one of the possessions I would bring to New York City with me when I moved there four years later.

The Shakespearean Tarot ignited a lifelong passion for and fascination with the artistry and design of Tarot cards. I love poring over them and contemplating how each artist has interpreted the symbolism. I particularly love the artwork of Pamela Colman Smith, who created the popular Rider-Waite-Smith deck. I visited the fabulous retrospective of her work at the Pratt Institute in January 2019, which included an analysis of her illustrations for the Tarot deck.

Moreover, as a writer, I love Tarot's storytelling element. The Tarot reader Laetitia Barbier once aptly described her profession to me as "poetic counseling." I enjoy listening to how each Tarot reader interprets the cards and how they weave a narrative thread around them. Fundamentally, Tarot readings are storytelling, and, given the scarcity of affordable entertainment in the nineteenth century, one could imagine that some of those seeking readings in that era were simply looking for a fun and relaxing way to spend their free time.

There is also something therapeutic about Tarot readings. Don't most people love being on the receiving end of attention? Many women (and men, for that matter) living on the Lower East Side were newly arrived immigrants trying to navigate life in a new country, and they were often in need of guidance. Some were simply seeking out the advice of someone who had life experience to offer. Since psychotherapy had not yet been invented, Tarot readings were one of the few ways working- and middle-class people could seek out and obtain advice, as well as solace and companionship. I saw these aspects of fortune telling in action as I watched the television show *The Marvelous Mrs. Maisel*. In the scenes between Miriam's mother and her fortune teller of choice, the visits would commence with the fortune teller glancing at her crystal ball, telling Miriam's mother everything was going to be OK, and then they would kvetch about their neighbors and watch television.

But who were the people seeking out readings in the era of Doesticks? Typically, the fortune tellers in the Doesticks book and those advertising in the newspapers charged between fifty cents and two dollars per reading, a significant sum for a working person then. In his chapter on fortune tellers in *Secrets of the Great City* (1868), James Dabney McCabe posited that the majority of those who sought out fortune tellers were gullible servant girls.[4] But consider that a female domestic with board in New York would make an average of $1.05 a week in 1850 and worked about sixteen hours a day. It is difficult to imagine how they found the time or the money to visit fortune tellers. This suggests that those who sought a reading were more likely middle class.

Furthermore, it seems that those who went to readings in that era believed these storytellers to be sincere about their profession and were also sympathetic to their need to make a living. Take, for example, the 1849 biography of Madame Rockwell, who had served as a fortune teller at Barnum's Museum for five years when the book was published. The anonymous biographer wrote that Madame Rockwell had an "unpretending air" and did not show "the least exterior sign of imposture." Such a portrayal demonstrates much more understanding of and sympathy for the life of a fortune teller than that of Doesticks. The author also observed that Madame Rockwell charged an "extremely reasonable price of twenty-five cents" and elaborated that she was working "for the bread of herself and family, following, in a business-like way, the poor trade of fortune-teller;— this woman is a PROPHETESS, whom Jeremiah would have honored and loved as a sister of Miriam—a daughter of Elijah."[5] When the biographer went for their first reading with Rockwell, the fortune teller intuited the person was to be her biographer. So, it seems that in that era there were some fortune tellers who genuinely believed they were seers and clients who to some degree believed in their power.

The term "fortune telling" was used with greater frequency in the newspapers beginning in the 1850s, during a period of rapid change. The steam-powered penny press had led to a great increase in the number of newspaper readers, and the information, opinion, and fiction published in those newspapers was fueled by the recent invention of the telegraph and developments in the field of photography. Experiments with electricity and magnetism were also becoming more sophisticated. Cities were growing, and the increasingly urban culture spurred many social changes. People may have started considering fortune tellers to be one of the many new and viable avenues of advice and information now available to them.

With the changes in technology and society in the 1850s came those who were questioning the dominant religions of the day and looking for alternatives to what they perceived as the harsh, structured, and judgmental Christian religion. Experts on the spiritualism movement often state that its roots grew from a variety of influences and philosophers, from the "Seer of Poughkeepsie," Andrew Jackson Davis, to Emanuel Swedenborg and Franz Anton Mesmer. The popularity of spiritualism in the United States would really gain momentum in 1848, with the Fox Sisters, who were believed to be able to communicate with the dead. Katie and Maggie Fox were living in Rochester, New York, when they heard the rappings of a peddler who had been murdered and buried in the basement. They called him "Mr. Splitfoot." The remarkable discovery of these young women instituted at spiritualism's core the belief that the living could speak with the dead. A noteworthy aspect of this movement was that it was predominantly female led. The belief at the time was that women, most particularly teenage girls, were more passive and therefore better conduits through which to receive messages from the dead. Women could also leverage this belief to gain agency and a speaking position in a society where they were otherwise allowed none.

Mainly women, but also men, sought out female practitioners for advice that was dispensed in the form of messages from beyond the grave. Some scholars have also suggested that spiritualism and fortune telling foreshadowed psychotherapy. After all, what were those who sought out fortune tellers, palm readers, and spiritualists essentially looking for? Peace of mind, guidance, and reassurance. To the sensibilities of the 1850s, these were characteristics associated with women, and therefore female practitioners were considered more desirable for this kind of work.

Of course, the rising interest and commitment to such practices as spiritualism and fortune telling were seen by some as a threat to the Christian church. Rather than lining up to confess to a priest, people were clamoring to receive advice and words of wisdom from a fortune teller or a spiritualist. They were likely less judgmental. Perhaps what ultimately interested and guided the likes of Doesticks was an investment in holding up the patriarchal pillars of the church, headed by men like his friend Henry Ward Beecher. In his attempt to expose fortune tellers, he seems to have sought out the least skilled and the most impoverished, those who were practicing mostly out of a need to make money, because so few other opportunities were available to them.

Doesticks was hardly the first or the last writer to mock spiritualists and clairvoyants. He existed within a tradition of male writers who swiftly responded to the burgeoning spiritualist movement with comic writing, which included James Russell Lowell's 1851 short story "The Unhappy Lot of Mr. Knott," Herman Melville's "The Apple-Tree Table" (1856), and Artemus Ward's "Among the Spirits" (1858). Moreover, just three years before the release of Doesticks's *New-York Tribune* articles, the *New York Times* had sent another reporter to investigate the fortune tellers of the Lower East Side, and that anonymous reporter's satiric and hyperbolic style was close to that of Doesticks.

As well as taking a revealing look at the fortune tellers and the people who frequented them, *Mortimer and the Witches* will also investigate the peculiar biography of Mortimer Thomson, who was guarding some shady secrets of his own and whose life in some ways paralleled the lives of the witches he visited and judged. While he would suffer challenges to his income, health, partnerships, and family relations, he was also a complicated man who would take heroic risks in his own life for the benefit of others.

It is hard to know whether Doesticks's descriptions of his subjects were entirely accurate; we can assume that in his disguise as the "Cash

Customer" he was not openly taking field notes. In his articles, he would have been describing his sessions from memory. Moreover, Doesticks appeared to be ignorant about Tarot and its history and paid little attention to details such as the types of deck the fortune tellers were using. However, most of the visuals, but not all, do correspond with those images depicted in the Lenormand deck, such as the moon, the snake, the coffin, the woman, the man, and the rider, all of which he notes when he describes the deck of Madame Clifton.[6] The subtitle of each chapter of *Mortimer and the Witches* uses the name of a Lenormand card and is framed by the card's meaning.

Lenormand cards appear around 1799; they were the cards of choice for Europeans for most of the latter part of the nineteenth century. Lenormand cards differ significantly from the seventy-eight-card Tarot decks commonly in use today. There are only thirty-six cards in a Lenormand deck. The symbolism tends to be straightforward, for example, a child, flowers, a bear, or keys. The deck's name comes from the famous French fortune teller Marie Anne Adelaide Lenormand. It was thought that a deck with her name would help it sell. Legend has it she was an advisor to Josephine Bonaparte, Maximilien Robespierre, and Jean-Paul Marat. Mademoiselle Lenormand liked to tell the story that she had advised Emperor Napoleon he would ultimately be unsuccessful in his military conquests, which motivated him to imprison her in the Bastille. The Lenormand deck was likely used by the fortune tellers discussed in this book.

Chapter 1

ılı

Madame Morrow

Lenormand Card: Book (Meaning = *Secrets*)

Madame Morrow offered an unusual challenge to Q. K. Philander Doesticks, P.B., as she was adamant in her advertisements that gentlemen would not be admitted to her salon.[1] In order to visit this famed witch, "*Astonishing to All*," as she had dubbed herself, Doesticks would have to disguise himself as a lady. He therefore proposed to dress himself up in a way that "would slightly astonish the Madame herself."[2] Madame Morrow was one of the most notorious "witches" and therefore worth the trouble, he surmised.

Casting off his gentlemanly garb, he began donning the complicated fashions of a lady, only to realize that the requisite "laces, ribbons, strings, bones, buttons, pins, capes, collars, and other inexplicable articles" were all too mysterious for a bachelor in his mid-twenties. He called upon his married friends from his theatrical past, and a great struggle and flurry to dress Doesticks in contemporary women's clothing ensued. The men pondered the problem of his short hair and disguised it by having him wear an elaborate bonnet. Amid this bustle and mayhem was the sudden realization among the men that they had forgotten to shave off Doesticks's mustache. Having already gone to the trouble of dressing up in this knotty clothing, Doesticks accepted that a trip to the barber was now out of the question. One of his friends would have to shave his mustache at arm's length, at which point he wrote that his head "looked as if it had been parboiled and the skin taken off."[3] As Doesticks caught sight of himself in the mirror, he was shocked to see that his image rendered him a little too like his landlady.

As the reporter ventured into the Lower East Side of 1857, he would have had to muscle his way through a vibrant city crowded with throngs of newsboys, peddlers ringing the bells of their pushcarts, knife grinders, men selling buckets of freshly shucked oysters, hot corn girls, and apple sellers. He likely passed businesses that included blacksmiths, tailors, apothecaries, shoemakers, hatters, breweries, print and machine shops, saloons, furniture and piano factories, and brick makers. The streets would have been an assault to the senses, with the smell of decomposing garbage; the blood, fear, and death emanating from slaughterhouses; decaying wharves; horse dung; and sewage spilling from poorly designed pipes. Doesticks would also have strolled by an intensely diverse range of ethnicities and nationalities, including Jews, Irish, Germans, Chinese, and African Americans.

And of course, Doesticks was attempting to navigate these streets dressed in a lady's restrictive garments, bedecked in petticoats, ribbons, and bows. He almost capsized stepping out onto the street, colliding with a young boy schlepping a wheelbarrow, who also managed to unravel a yard of lace from Doesticks's skirt.[4]

In the case of each witch that he visited, Doesticks provided detailed and gut-wrenching descriptions of the neighborhood. "Filth" and "dirt" were his staple adjectives when describing the Lower East Side. Madame Morrow's environs on Broome Street were no exception. She was said to live in a squat, three-story brick house. According to Doesticks, the area was populated by thieves, and sunshine was his only protection. There was some accuracy in that statement. Madame Morrow resided not too far from the city's Five Points neighborhood, a densely populated, disease-ridden, crime-infested slum, whose notoriety has spread to this century with Martin Scorsese's 2002 film *Gangs of New York*. Charles Dickens also famously wrote of the horrors of the neighborhood in his *American Notes*, when he visited in 1842. In 1857, the year Doesticks wrote his original articles for the *Tribune*, George Templeton Strong would also write in his diary that there had been an "epidemic of crime this winter." In the same way that Doesticks wrote about the fortune tellers, men of privilege would often visit the Five Points and describe it in a way that sensationalized the poverty and offered more a reflection of the writer's anxieties than empathetic writing that might propel change.

Upon ringing Madame Morrow's doorbell, Doesticks was admitted by a young Irish lady, likely a servant, and he observed two small children (a common presence in the witches' living quarters). The Irish greeter ushered Doesticks into the parlor, which he noted was small and contained a huge basket brimming with soiled linen. Doesticks guessed that the laundry must be from a respectable family. A sign on the wall informed him he must pay one dollar for a ticket to see Madame Morrow.

Doesticks waited for an hour and a half to see the famed "seventh daughter of a seventh daughter." No other customers were noted to enter during that time. It can only be speculated as to what Madame Morrow might have been doing during the waiting period. Was she with another customer? Was she in the middle of another job, such as dressmaking? Was she busy completing her own domestic chores? Was she out of the building and only made aware of her "Cash Customer" once she arrived home? While stuck in the waiting room, Doesticks overheard gossip between the two washerwomen regarding the merits of engines No. 18 and 27—as well as of the handsome men of the related fire department.

The Irish girl then invited Doesticks to the room of Madame Morrow. He walked up a narrow flight of stairs, which he judged to be dirty, of course, and then was guided into what he felt was an elegantly furnished parlor. He described Madame Morrow as looking tall and sallow, with skin the complexion of "old parchment." He also noted her light brown eyes and that she was dressed in half-mourning.

From the front parlor, Madame Morrow guided her strange female client to a closet-like room with two chairs and a table holding handbills and a pack of cards. She asked Doesticks's month of birth, and with that small amount of information, consulted a book (Doesticks didn't observe the title) and told her guest that "she" was amiable and frank, a desirable marriage partner, and that "her" lucky days were Tuesdays and Thursdays.

After this series of generalized statements, Madame Morrow took up the pack of cards and began shuffling and cutting. She then laid out the cards and rapidly fired off a series of cliched assertions and crowd-pleasing statements such as "You face luck, you face prosperity, you face true love," and so forth. Doesticks seemed amused by Madame Morrow's prediction that he faced "two gentlemen with a view to matrimony, one of whom has brown hair and brown eyes, and the other has lighter hair and blue eyes."[5] One can almost hear him snickering to himself at Madame Morrow's proclamations.

At the end of the reading, Madame Morrow invited the lady to view the visage of her future husband. With women being for the most part so utterly dependent economically on their husbands, a fortune teller's young and (mostly) single guests would be greatly interested in catching a glimpse of their prospective spouses. Madame Morrow took what was then defined as a "magic mirror" out of a pine box. She dramatically drew aside a little curtain, and Doesticks observed "an indistinct figure of a bloated face with a mustache, with black eyes and black hair; it was a hang-dog, thief-like face, and one that he would not have passed in the street without involuntarily putting his hands on his pockets to assure himself that all was right."[6]

Disappointed by this vision, Doesticks delivered an aside to the reader that a magic mirror could be procured from any optician for a dollar and a quarter and that the vision of the husband-to-be was easily varied by swapping the picture at one end of the instrument. He paid Madame Morrow for this depressing vision and swiftly bade her adieu.

Doesticks noted that on his return home he had to "cut himself out of his unaccustomed harness by the help of a pen-knife with a file-blade."[7] It was as much of a struggle to remove his lady disguise as it had been to heave himself into it.

Even as Mortimer Thomson attempted to discredit Madame Morrow as a charlatan and former prostitute, he had his own shadowy past.

Thomson was born on September 2, 1831,[8] in Riga, New York, a tiny hamlet with a population of fewer than 3,500 at the time. It was approximately sixty-two miles east of Niagara Falls and seventeen miles west of Rochester, not too far from where the Fox sisters first heard rappings. The first postmaster of Riga was Joseph Thompson (sic), who is likely to have been Mortimer Thomson's grandfather.[9] Thomson's mother was Sophia Edna Thomson, who was noted in her obituary for writing poetry under the pseudonym "Rosamond." His mother had selected her sons' names from plays: Mortimer's from Richard Cumberland's *The Fashionable Lover* and his younger brother Clifford's from James Sheridan Knowles's *The Hunchback*.[10] Thomson's father, Edwin, was a lawyer.[11] Thomson therefore seems to have grown up in a comfortable, educated, and middle-class family, which might have made him unsympathetic to the plight of struggling working-class and immigrant women. Clifford went on to be a journalist and editor, just like Mortimer, and the brothers were close, often working at the same newspapers together.[12]

An obituary of Mortimer Thomson by his fellow humorist Eli Perkins (real name, Melville D. Landon) in the *Inter Ocean* offers this account of him as a young boy:

In 1840 Mortimer Thompson [*sic*] was a queer, gaunt, eccentric, cadaverous nine-year-old boy in the city of Rochester. He was always up to strange tricks in his early childhood, keeping his parents, who were in ordinary circumstances, constantly excited as to his safety. The tricks he played upon older people, such as tripping them over wires stretched across the sidewalk in the twilight, etc., frequently resulted in chasings and kicking abroad, and hair-pullings and hand-cuffings at home.[13]

When he was about nine years old, the family left for Minnesota, and Thomson eventually enrolled in the University of Michigan. He did not complete his degree there, however, as he was expelled during the winter of his first term in 1849. Accounts vary as to the nature of Thomson's expulsion. One obituary tantalizingly claimed that he was expelled for "too much enterprise in securing subjects for the dissecting-room."[14] Yes! Doesticks was allegedly a grave robber, an occupation considered scandalous at the time, not only because of the secretive, murky actions a person would have to undergo to rob a body but also because it betrayed the ideal of a proper Christian death and was mortifying for the loved ones of the deceased.

Another report in the *New York Herald* attested, "His membership of a secret collegiate society precipitated his retirement before the anger of the Faculty."[15] According to the records of the University of Michigan, the latter account is the truth. What emerges from all these varying stories regarding the nature of Thomson's expulsion from the University of Michigan is a picture of a mischievous, rebellious, and lively young man with a rakish sense of humor.

Perhaps it is this penchant for pranks and drama that caused Thomson to take up with a traveling theater troupe that the *New York Herald* called a "romantic connection with a strolling company of players."[16] It may have been in this environment that Thomson picked up his taste for dressing up and playing the part, just as the fortune tellers were sure to have perfected the art of performing a convincing role of their own. Thomson had described himself as the "most numerous man of the troupe." There were only five in the company, and one night he assumed seven different roles in the play *Pizarro*.[17]

Becoming listless with his wandering theater friends, Thomson decided to settle in New York to meet what he proclaimed in an article in the persona of Doesticks as "the famous people of the great city." His New York beginnings were much less glamorous than that, as he moved to Brooklyn with his parents and friend Ed Wells and found a job as a clerk at Sackett,

Davis and Potter, a jewelry store near Broadway and Maiden Lane. He would also have to wait a couple of years before he could bring his betrothed over from the Midwest.

According to his 1875 obituary in the *Inter Ocean*, it was while Thomson was corresponding with Ed Wells that his talents were unleashed.[18] It was said that at a certain point in 1854, Wells gave one of Thomson's uproarious letters to the *Detroit Tribune*, an account of a drinking excursion to Niagara Falls. Another theory posits that the original letter was published in a student newspaper. The likelier story, however, is that the letters were first published in the *Detroit Advertiser* in 1854, where Thomson's brother Clifford was working at the time. In an article published in the *Evening Post*, Thomson had written:

> Doesticks is a modest young clerk in this city, whose life thus far has only spanned some twenty-three years, and he is disinclined, at present, to part with his anonymous obscurity. He has nothing to offer the publishers at present, and when he has, if ever, he thinks it will be time enough to reveal his whereabouts and whatabouts. He is not looking to literature as a profession, sees no literary merit in what he has done, writes to the *Advertiser* to oblige a younger brother who is connected with that journal, and for no other object.[19]

The letter titled "Doesticks on a Bender" was republished in numerous newspapers, and from there Thomson's fame under the guise of Q. K. Philander Doesticks, P.B., skyrocketed. At that point in US history, there were no copyright laws, and it was customary for newspapers to reprint articles and letters printed in other newspapers without the worry of having to pay the artist or the original publisher. Following the circulation of the Niagara Falls letter, rumors and gossip about the identity of this letter writer began to spread. According to Thomson's obituary in the *New York Times*, Charles Anderson Dana, the editor of the *New-York Tribune*, had begun publishing enough of Doesticks's letters to fill a page of his newspaper, and this caused the reading public to speculate as to the identity of the author. Dana eventually found Thomson, "a very green-looking, bashful youth, with the mere beginning of a beard on his chin; with long, dark brown hair, and an Indian cast of features,"[20] working as a petty clerk in the Maiden Lane jewelry establishment.[21]

Founded in 1841 by Horace Greeley, by the 1850s the *New-York Tribune* employed fifty people and was in a five-story building on Park Row. One of three main newspapers in New York City in the 1850s (the *New York Herald*, *New-York Tribune*, and *New York Times*), the *Tribune* was known for being mostly devoted to social justice causes. Once located by Dana, Thomson would be hired to cover theater, write more articles under his Doesticks pseudonym, and report on the police courts.

Dana's discovery of Thomson did not stop the chattering tongues of other speculating newspapers, who, like a bad fortune teller, continued their projections a year later. On November 25, 1854, for example, the *Buffalo Daily Republic* declared the identity of Doesticks a mystery and suggested that perhaps it was someone by the name of Morton who had recently taken a wife.[22]

More of Doesticks's capers were published in the newspapers over the course of 1854, including articles about Barnum's Museum, the quality of water from the Croton Aqueduct, commentary on churchgoing in New York City (scholars of Doesticks agree he was likely writing about Grace Church), and entertainment on the Bowery, among other things. Another article titled "Doesticks Invents a Patent Medicine" was a sendup of some of the wild patent medicine inventions of the era. In this case, it was a "Self-Acting-Four-Horse-Power Balsam," which was "designed to cure all diseases of mind, body, or estate, to give strength to the weak, money to the poor, bread and butter to the hungry, boots to the bare-foot, decency to blackguards, and common sense to the Know-Nothings."[23] Eventually, Thomson was approached by the publisher E. Livermore, who published his first book, *Doesticks What He Says*.

Reception of Thomson's work was mixed even before the book's publication. In February 1855, a correspondent for the *Albany Express* unfavorably compared the writing of Thomson's future mother-in-law, Fanny Fern, to Doesticks's, stating: "I don't know how it is in Albany, but it seems to me that 'Fanny Fern' is becoming a bore. You read nothing else, hear nothing else, but 'Ruth Hall' and the 'Ellet family.' 'Doesticks' had plenty of rope and verified the old adage."[24] The *Buffalo Commercial Advertiser* was positively disdainful of Thomson's work: "Any person who can write at all, and write grammatically, can ridicule the popular follies, and find readers, for mankind are more prone to listen to sarcasm and ridicule, applied to any subject, than to solid discussion or serious rebuke."[25] Another article in the same newspaper said, "It is difficult to perceive wherein consists the merit of this strangely named author. He perpetrates an abundance of nonsense, which is not redeemed by any novelty or wit, or even humor. Whatever capacity the person has for any line of authorship, he is throwing away upon these essays, which, owing to the republication of them in the newspapers, he must imagine are equal to Thackeray and Dickens."[26]

His critics all seem to have agreed that Doesticks was wildly popular, and one of his supporters noted:

> This writer, by striking out and diligently working a new vein of humor and satire, has in half a year attained a wider popularity than writers in general can reasonably hope to acquire in ten times that period. His letters appear originally in the Detroit Daily Advertiser, but they are copied all over the country. The N.Y. Tribune recently paid them the extraordinary compliment of republishing the entire series in a single number of that paper, for which the demand was so great that ten thousand extra copies were sold.[27]

In May 1855, advertisements began appearing in the newspapers announcing the forthcoming book from the much-discussed Doesticks. Those of a suspicious disposition began questioning the appearance of articles announcing the death of Doesticks. On June 1, 1855, the *New-York Tribune* reported that Thomson had been killed in a shooting accident in Ann Arbor, Michigan.[28] News of Thomson's death spread quickly to other newspapers, which reprinted the *New-York Tribune* article, even though less than a week later it was announced that the whole thing was a hoax. On June 9, 1855, the *Times-Picayune* philosophized that it had been a stunt to publicize the upcoming Doesticks book.[29] The *New-York Tribune* tried to wave the whole affair away, publishing a letter from Thomson, who joked that the sidekick of the Doesticks's articles, Damphool, must have been behind the whole affair.[30]

The book *Doesticks What He Says* was released in July 1855 to yet more varied reception. Just as Thomson would mock his fortune tellers for their lowbrow storytelling, the *Living Age* wrote, "It is written in a low, flash style, and its subjects, scenes and characters are about on a par with its literary pretensions. A 'Bowery boy' odor pervades the book throughout, and it is unfit for decent society."[31] The *Louisville Daily Courier* also wrote a short, dismissive review: "This is neither a history, romance, life-drama, biography, autobiography nor post mortem examination, but a series of unpremeditated literary extravaganzas, written without malice aforethought by the single hero thereof, purely for his own glorification, and printed and published solely for his own profit."[32]

In other words, Doesticks was only to be read by the masses. While some newspapers may have expressed contempt for the book's literary merits, the *Vermont Watchman and State Journal* praised how much his works were enjoyed: "Our readers have had a taste of Doesticks, and from that sample may safely judge of the whole invoice. Rich in the ridiculous or ridiculously rich, and of course provoking to the risibles. The book is well printed and illustrated."[33] The *Citizen* praised Doesticks's book, claiming: "This is one of the most amusing witty books published in this country for many years. It is full of fun and life, and o' keen satire, though of that good-natured kind that leaves no sting behind, but makes even the object of the ridicule laugh at himself."[34] Frequently quoted advance praise for the book came from the famous editor Nathaniel P. Willis (and coincidentally the brother of Thomson's future mother-in-law), who wrote, "Things so copied, so talked of, so pulled out of every pocket to be lent to you, so quoted and so relished and laughed over as Doestick's [*sic*] writings were launched into print."

Following the success of his first book, Doesticks would rapidly publish other successful works, including a poetical work, *Plu-ri-bus-tah*, in 1856, a literary burlesque of Longfellow's *The Song of Hiawatha*, which included a chapter mocking spiritualists, a common theme of the author's; *The History and Records of the Elephant Club*, also in 1856, a satire on New York City and its socialites coauthored with Edward Fitch Underhill; and a play, *The Lady of the Lake*, in 1860, which was performed at the famed Niblo's Garden.

Thomson's star had risen, and the future appeared to be blazing bright. However, he would not "face luck" for long—as Madame Morrow had predicted.

Of all the witches that Thomson wrote about, given her notoriety, Madame Morrow's life is to some extent the easiest to trace. These working-class women disguised the nature of their professions in the city directories and city census, possibly to evade the law. Unlike Thomson, they would not earn literary recognition or be commemorated with obituaries in the press and tombstones in noted and historic cemeteries. Besides advertisements or sensationalized details of their arrests, of which Madame Morrow had a few, these women rarely made it into the news.

Many of the women placed advertisements in local newspapers such as the *New York Herald*, *New-York Tribune*, *Brooklyn Daily Eagle*, *New York Times*, and even the *Spiritual Telegraph*, a newspaper in circulation from 1852 to 1860 and dedicated to all matters associated with spiritualism. New York really was a small town in the 1800s. The newspaper offices were located at 300 Broadway, a couple of doors down from one of Thomson's later book publishers, Rudd & Carleton.

The fortune tellers' advertisements tell us a lot about the wishes and dreams of New Yorkers of the time. Often the mediums would make grand and hyperbolic promises of curing ailments and advise on business, love, and marriage. Further, the multitude of missing husbands in the mid-to-late nineteenth century and early twentieth century is a rarely discussed phenomenon, but some psychics also laid claim to being able to locate lost husbands, most famously a man by the name of Abraham Hochman, referred to as "The Richest Man on Rivington Street" at the turn of the twentieth century. Thanks to Hochman's affordable fees and high success rates, the press often reported he was trailed by "wildly gesticulating women."[35] This prevalence of missing husbands—men who became overwhelmed by the pressure of raising large families and would abandon them—can also explain the desperation of women who turned to fortune telling for either advice or as a source of regular income.

Madame Morrow was among the most famous in her trade. Even one of Doesticks's peers, the illustrator Thomas Butler Gunn, wrote about her in his book *The Physiology of New York Boarding-Houses*, in a chapter titled "The Boarding-House Where There Are Marriageable Daughters." Gunn wrote, "All three will admit that they have been to Madame Morrow's to have their fortunes told."[36]

Madame Morrow's advertisements started appearing in local newspapers in February 1854, and news of her arrest swiftly followed. The first account appeared in June 1854 in several Brooklyn newspapers, including the *Brooklyn Daily Eagle* and the *Brooklyn Free Press*. It was noted that she was living at No. 76 Broome Street. She was arrested by Officer De Binder of the Third District Police Court for defrauding Ann Crawley, who lived at No. 254 Marshall Street in Brooklyn. Crawley, like Doesticks, had been repulsed by the appearance of her future husband, shown to her by the fortune teller through a glass, for a fee of one dollar. Subsequently, Crawley had reported Madame Morrow to the police. Madame Morrow was forced to pay a fine of three hundred dollars and make a promise of good behavior, which would not last very long—advertisements for her services reappeared in the newspapers soon after the incident.

The original statute for prosecuting fortune telling in New York was created in 1819 and revised in 1861. It was hashed together in a law that also prosecuted those who abandoned and neglected to support wives or children or threatened to run away or leave their wives or children; it also penalized prostitution, gambling, and, bizarrely, juggling, performing puppet shows, and wire or rope dancing. It ultimately decreed that those practicing any of these transgressions "shall be deemed disorderly persons."

The second time Madame Morrow was arrested, it was reported, among others, by Thomson himself in the *New-York Tribune*. In October 1858, he would have been busily getting ready to promote the publication of his upcoming book in December. Thomson concluded his account of Madame Morrow's arrest by stating: "The book will be looked for with increased interest because of this first attempt to break up the illegal business."[37] Attempting to take credit for the legal dismantling of the fortune telling business was deceitful of Thomson. Other newspapers had been documenting these local arrests for several years.

Other articles in the *New York Times* and the *Alton Daily Courier* offer more dramatic and detailed accounts. Somebody had sent a circular of Madame Morrow's to Mayor Daniel F. Tiemann, complaining that she was a nuisance, and the mayor had sent one Sergeant Croft to investigate. Upon arrival at Madame Morrow's residence at 46 Norfolk Street, Croft had been refused service by her in the waiting room, because he was a man, but he told her she was under arrest nonetheless. Customers in waiting started screaming and running, but Croft reassured them that the fortune teller was the only one among them who would be arrested. She was taken, along with her husband and servant, to the Fourth Ward station house, close to the river on the Lower East Side, and locked up overnight. In the morning, she was brought before the mayor, who read her the statute and told her she had violated the law. She was fined five hundred dollars, which was paid for by her mother, and once again made to promise good behavior and abstinence from fortune telling. Madame Morrow would again promptly break her vows, as her advertisements continued to appear in newspapers in the months and years following.

It is little wonder that she returned to fortune telling. If newspaper estimates are correct, she was making between fifty and seventy-five dollars per day.[38] Moreover, according to the New York City directory, Madame Morrow reported that her income came from dressmaking, one of very few employment options available to women. Female seamstresses made as little as seventy-five cents a week; Madame Morrow could make that in just one reading.

There are many accounts in books and newspapers of the time about the hardship of seamstresses in New York City. They were not always single women but might be women who had to make a living for their families, perhaps because they had been abandoned by their husband or had a husband who was a drunk or physically incapacitated and unable to work. The work of seamstresses paid a pittance and left women in the most desperate of circumstances. It was also brutally taxing work on the body. The economist and social reformer Virginia Penny wrote that she could recognize a seamstress on the street simply by her stooped carriage, "the neck suddenly bending forward, and the arms being, even in walking, considerably bent forward, or folded more or less upward from the elbows."[39] The author Fanny Fern would also highlight in her novel *Ruth Hall* the difficulties of the work of a seamstress when her formerly middle-class heroine was left destitute by her family and made to find women's work. Fern wrote: "'Only fifty-cents for all this ruffling and hemming,' said Ruth, as she picked up the wick of her dim lamp; 'only fifty cents! and I have labored diligently too, every spare moment, for a fortnight; this will never do.'"[40]

For an example of the desperate straits women of the time could find themselves in, two sisters, Cecelia and Wanda Stein, immigrated to New York from Germany in 1852. They were both single, and Wanda was the mother of an illegitimate child. In 1855, while they were working as embroiderers, their employer went out of business. They were unable to find other employment, and the rent was due. They had no food. Perhaps the only option left to them at this point was prostitution, which one might assume was not a desirable choice for the sisters, so they went to bed with the six-year-old child and committed suicide by ingesting prussic acid, a bitter-tasting, fast-acting form of cyanide, which inhibits oxygen use at the cellular level and causes hypoxia. It was discovered by a Swedish chemist in 1782 who was preparing it for Prussian blue, a pigment. By 1829, a statute had been passed in New York State emphasizing that prussic acid must be labeled as poison, so there can be little doubt regarding the intention of the sisters.

Madame Morrow's poverty is further highlighted by the number of times she moved. Her addresses throughout the years included 184 Ludlow Street in New York City, with other brief listings at 331 Grayson Street, Louisville, Kentucky; 156 Baronne Street, Lafayette, Louisiana; and 75 Pleasant Street, Falls River, Massachusetts. She was also arrested in Pittsburgh in June 1859, where she had been practicing under several aliases, including "Madam Willis" and "Madame B." When her house was searched, books were found on palmistry, fortune telling, and dreams, as well as others of more "questionable character," whatever that may mean. Officers also found pictures of young men who were promised to other young women by the matchmaking astrologer. Two letters were found, one from a young man asking for a suitable bride and another from a Mrs. E. Robinson, dated October 1858, whose friend Miss Fannie Bennett had recommended the services of Madame Morrow. Mrs. Robinson had promptly sent Madame Morrow five dollars for her services but had never heard back from the clairvoyant. Several days later, a letter in the *Pittsburg Gazette* from Mrs. E. Robinson expressed insult at the association with Madame Morrow, stating that her letter was fabricated and accusing the newspaper of attacking her character.

The *Pittsburg Gazette* offered further background on Madame Morrow, including that her real name was Mrs. Elizabeth Morris and that she had a husband called Isaac. He had escaped before Madame Morrow was arrested and could not be found. The newspaper also offered that her maiden name was Elizabeth Westby and that she was a native of Philadelphia.

The *Gazette* claimed that the local police had been more successful in capturing fortune tellers than the New York police. Madame Morrow was apparently fined twenty-five dollars but had also been told to leave the city within twenty-four hours. She must have done so, because within a matter of months she was advertising in the New York papers again and did for some years following.

The *Brooklyn Daily Eagle*, which had printed the first account of one of Madame Morrow's arrests, also presented what appeared to be the final advertisement on record for Madame Morrow on October 18, 1876: "Madame Morrow, independent clairvoyant, by request of her friends will remain for two weeks longer at 808 Myrtle av. She will tell of past, present and future, describes absent friends, lost property, and treats diseases of every nature."[41] Coincidentally, Madame Morrow had been telling fortunes at a temporary address in Brooklyn not far from where Thomson resided in the late 1850s.

Two years before this Brooklyn advertisement, Madame Morrow's name appeared in the press in connection with the first kidnapping case involving ransom to receive widespread media coverage in the United States. On July 1, 1874, two young boys, Charles Brewster Ross, age four, and his older brother Walter, age six, were playing outside their upper-middle-class home in Philadelphia. A century before "stranger danger" warnings, two men in a carriage pulled up and offered the boys candy and fireworks if they would come for a ride with them. They were driven for about eight miles to a store. Walter was sent in to buy treats, and when he came out, Charley, as he was more commonly known, and the men were gone. Christian K. Ross, the boys' father, who had lost almost all his money in the Panic of 1873, began receiving ransom notes for his boy. He went to the police and also solicited the services of the Pinkerton Detective Agency. The story became a sensation in the news, and popular songs and plays were written about the crime. Sightings of Charley came in from all over the United States.

In August of that year, the police got their break, and they began searching for two criminals: William Mosher, a Long Island boat builder and ex-convict, and Joseph Douglas. They were being protected by William Westervelt, Mosher's brother-in-law, who was a former policeman. Charley's father died in 1897, and although on a few occasions the police had come close, the crime was never solved, though many people came forward in the twentieth century claiming to be Charley.

With regards to Madame Morrow, in December 1874, Westervelt and Douglas were wandering around the Lower East Side, where Mosher was waiting in a local saloon on Allen and Houston Street. Westervelt testified at the trial that Douglas had walked across the street to visit Madame Morrow.[42] Her sons Ed and Ike were alleged to be long-time acquaintances of the Mosher brothers, and it was also claimed that the kidnappers liked to have their fortunes told by the famed clairvoyant.

Douglas came back to the saloon and told Mosher that Gil (Mosher's brother) had been looking for him at Madame Morrow's. Mosher rushed across the street to query Madame Morrow regarding the whereabouts of his brother. Fifteen minutes later, Mosher returned crying and cursing, demanding that Westervelt go to Gil's house with a letter. Westervelt obtained paper, pen, and ink from the bartender, and Mosher dictated a letter to Westervelt, stating that he had no idea what Gil wanted from him and that he had no time to meet him or money to spend. If Gil wanted to see him, he must explain what he wanted. Westervelt agreed to take the letter to Gil. When Westervelt visited Liz Mosher (Mosher's sister-in-law and Gil's wife), she informed Westervelt that the police suspected William of kidnapping Charley Ross.

Mosher and Douglas died in a shootout attempting to burgle the home of Judge Charles Van Brunt in Bay Ridge, Brooklyn, on December 13, 1874. The previous night, they had met in a group at the home of Madame Morrow. Doesticks seems to have been correct in his assessment that Madame Morrow hung out with disreputable sorts.

Around the time of her probable death (since her advertisements stopped appearing in the press), Madame Morrow would make one more court appearance, in name at least. Cornelius Vanderbilt, aka "the Commodore," the shipping and railroad magnate, passed away in January 1877. Three of his children contested his will, unhappy with what they perceived to be the paltry sum he had left them. They claimed their father was not in his right mind when he had drawn up the will, and the main basis of their argument was that their father had consulted with corrupt spiritu-alists, a clear indication that he had dementia and was susceptible to sin-ister influences.[43] In October 1878, Mrs. Helen C. Stille testified that the Commodore had told her sometime in the early 1860s that he had great confidence in the predictions of one Madame Morrow, a lady who had been born with a caul over her face and the seventh daughter of a seventh daughter, both clear indications of her spiritual powers, to his thinking. He urged Mrs. Stille to accompany him on his next visit to Madame Morrow to witness her "extraordinary powers." This story was presented as evidence that Vanderbilt was clearly deluded in his final years.

There are no traceable records of Madame Morrow's death. As she was an impoverished Lower East Side woman, an obituary in the newspaper or a tombstone at a celebrated cemetery was never in the cards.

Madame Morrow's name would live on in other ways. In 1867, a deck of "Madame Morrow's Fortune Telling Cards" was published as a replica of the Berlin Kunst-Comptoir deck of 1854. In 1886, a new edition was copyrighted. That deck remains in circulation and is still used today.

Chapter 2

Madame Clifton

Lenormand Card: Garden (Meaning = *Socializing*)

Doesticks felt sure he had caught Madame Clifton red handed.[1] Spreading gossip like a gleeful busybody, he asserted that a "finely moustached" gentleman was exiting the door of Madame Clifton's establishment as he arrived. He then surmised that the gentleman must be there on business of a salacious nature. It was highly improbable that this gentleman, he thought, was simply seeking a reading.

Madame Clifton resided at No. 185 Orchard Street, just a little south of Houston Street. Doesticks noted there was nothing orchard-like about Orchard Street. Instead, he observed a motley-colored assortment of low brick houses, "seedy" in appearance. The local businesses were a black-smith, a paint room, and a livery stable. Like some of the other houses inhabited by the witches, Madame Clifton's was a two-story red brick house with green window blinds, but she may have been better off than her comrades, as Doesticks said her tenement was kept in good repair.

Doesticks approved of the neat-looking "colored" girl who answered the door and asked if he understood Madame Clifton's terms. Doesticks then insinuated that had he not been clear about his purpose of business, the servant would most certainly have assumed he was there to take advantage of prostitution services offered by the madame. How did Doesticks have such ready knowledge of how brothels were operated? Perhaps, being a bachelor at the time of writing, he frequented them himself. It was common in the nineteenth century for women employed in sex work to be harshly judged by society, yet the men who frequented these houses of ill repute were not.

Learning that Doesticks was there to have his fortune read, the servant withdrew to inform the mistress, leaving Doesticks alone to dispense his judgments upon the sitting room, which in a rare instance was not pronounced "filthy" but rather "neatly-finished." The room even contained a piano. There was also, inexplicably, a huge signboard for a perfume store, which was not very witch-like, in his opinion. As he pondered the purpose of the sign, the servant reentered and in a low voice invited Doesticks to follow her up two flights of stairs into a room where a large glass case was filled with a stock of perfumes.

On a small stand were two packs of cards. One pack was an ordinary playing deck; the other was a deck of fortune telling cards. Doesticks's detailed descriptions of the simple symbols of the deck, such as a moon, a snake, and a man on horseback, suggests that Madame Clifton was likely using Lenormand cards.

Doesticks did not indicate how long he waited for the madame, only that she soon appeared. He judged her to be a fine but average-looking woman, about thirty-five years old (though it should be noted that thirty-five was the average age estimate for almost all the witches he encountered), with steel-blue eyes and black hair. With her thick eyebrows, Doesticks surmised she was giving him a menacing look. He also deemed her to have a "fake" smile and "false" voice, casting doubt on the madame even before she had begun her reading. Doesticks compared her to a "smiling cat," a predator ready to pounce. In fact, throughout the reading he would liken her gestures and movements to that of a cat.

Madame Clifton swiftly commenced shuffling the cards and laid them out in three rows face up. She told Doesticks of his history, all of which he wrote was blatantly false, without going into detail. Perhaps observing that Doesticks looked unconvinced, she began asking him questions about his past. He confessed to being a bachelor but refused to give much more information than that.

The tone of the reading took a darker turn as Madame Clifton perceived her guest to be skeptical and uncooperative. She began predicting a horrifying future for Doesticks, with every conceivable kind of terror. Seeing he was startled, she told Doesticks she was required to tell him what she saw in the cards, that she must be truthful. He would have disappointment in business, one of his dearest friends (or perhaps a relative) would die, and he would fall ill from a weakness in the chest and lungs.

Moreover, he did not have an agreeable personality. He was impulsive, proud, ambitious, and quick-tempered, and these characteristics would aggravate all kinds of illnesses and disease, to the point that she was beginning to fear he was the one who would be buried, rather than his friend or relative. Doesticks loved a "light-complexioned" lady, but her friends did not approve. A "dark-complexioned" man was trying to take this lady away from him. If Doesticks wasn't careful, this man would do great injury to him. Madame Clifton also predicted a journey, one of trouble, misfortune, grief, sorrow, and loss.

Having pronounced this gloomy prophecy, the madame then attempted to guess the real name of Doesticks to demonstrate her mastery in mind reading, but apparently did not guess a single letter right. Feeling like she might be losing her client's trust entirely, she attempted to distract Doesticks by predicting even more bad luck for him, to the point that Doesticks "began almost to fear that he would break his leg before he rose from his chair, or would instantly fall down in a fit and be carried off to die at the Hospital."[2]

It was then that the madame revealed her showpiece. She told Doesticks if he put his trust in her, his fate could be changed. If he would buy her "Chinese Ruling Planet Charm," which she had imported from China at great expense, he could remove all his bad luck. The charm was worth somewhere between five and fifty dollars (that's a cool $1,700+ in 2023), but since Doesticks was clearly doomed, he would have to pay full price for the charm to thwart his upcoming onslaught of horrible luck. Madame Clifton proceeded to tell stories of husbands and wives who had been apart for three years but were brought back together after wearing the charm. She assured Doesticks that he could not possibly die if he were to wear it. In reply, Doesticks told Madame Clifton that he did not have fifty dollars on him to purchase immortality but that after he received his year's salary he would be sure to call again.

Madame Clifton then said, "If you happen to call when I am engaged, tell the girl to say that you want to see me about *medicine*, and I will see you, for I never put off anybody who wants *medicine*, no matter who is with me, say *medicine*, and I will see you instantly."[3] Clearly, *medicine* was code that Madame Clifton was about to make a great deal of money and that she should drop everything to attend to whoever was calling. As he exited, Doesticks could not help stretching his imagination, speculating what kind of *medicine* the madame might be prepared to furnish for her clientele upon a second visit.

▌▌▌

As much as Thomson derided the activities of Madame Clifton, he loved to socialize with bohemian characters he might have otherwise deemed unsavory, had they not been born into the veneer of middle-class respectability. Shortly after Thomson's arrival in the city of New York, he became a frequenter of the German beer cellar Pfaff's.

Pfaff's was located on the eastern edge of Greenwich Village, initially at 647 Broadway, a short walk from Madame Clifton's, and was known for attracting a literary and artistic clientele. It is considered by some scholars to be one of the first bohemian bars in the United States, modeled on similar establishments in France. One of the most illustrious frequenters of Pfaff's was Walt Whitman. Other patrons included artists who are lesser known today but celebrated in their time, among them the essayist, poet, and journalist George Arnold; the actor Edwin Booth (brother of Lincoln's assassin); Charles Constant Delmonico, the restaurateur; the artist Winslow Homer; and the actress and temptress Lola Montez. They considered Edgar Allan Poe to be their bohemian inspiration and a kind of patron saint.

The gathering was inspired by Henry Clapp Jr., who had recently witnessed bohemians during a visit to Paris, and he longed to set up a similar community of his own in New York City. He found the ideal place in the establishment of Charles Ignatius Pfaff, the proprietor, who was often described as a rotund, generous, welcoming man, accepting of all his quirky customers. Born in Baden, Switzerland, of German descent, he arrived in New York in the 1850s, along with a wave of other German immigrants. Pfaff apparently had impeccable taste in German beer, fine wines, and champagnes, and he served excellent coffee. His establishment even offered full meals that included *pfannkuchen* (a hearty German pancake), Welsh rarebit (an open-faced grilled cheese sandwich with a sauce composed of beer, cheese, butter, and mustard), liver with bacon, beef steak, and a cheese plate.

Pfaff's was a classic German beer cellar, modeled on the *Ratskellers* of the proprietor's native country. When Thomson walked up to Pfaff's, he would have seen the word *Pfaff* faintly lettered on the Coleman House hotel's gray brick exterior, and he would have descended a stairway to the basement, where ample wooden tables and chairs accommodated the throngs of lively artists who frequented the saloon. Lit with gas lamps, the establishment was broad and wide, with low ceilings and a sawdust-covered floor.

Partly thanks to its walking proximity to Newspaper Row, Pfaff's attracted many journalists besides Thomson. One can imagine him to be a popular patron of the establishment. As his daughter once said of him, "He had a peculiar aptitude for winning not only the friendship but often the almost romantic devotion of other men."[4] Perhaps this devotion was inspired by Thomson's love of pranks and good liquor. One posthumous article that appeared in the *Vicksburg Evening Post* on May 30, 1910, told of Thomson's tendency for mischief at work and at large. King Edward VII, the Prince of Wales and in his late teens at the time, was visiting the United States in 1860 under the charge of the Duke of Newcastle. The prince was watched closely by the newspaper men of the day. Among those assigned were none other than Mortimer Thomson and George F. Williams, from the *New York Times*. One day during the prince's visit, the Duke of Newcastle was called away while Thomson and Williams were waiting for the royal party in their apartments at a Fifth Avenue hotel. The prince, now alone with Thomson and Williams, told them that he was bored by all the official receptions and wished to experience the "real" New York anonymously, without his royal attendants. Thomson suggested that this was just the time for them to slip away. The prince enthusiastically agreed and followed Thomson and Williams along a back route out of the hotel.

The newspapermen took the prince on a tour around Union Square and other nearby areas, including a stop at one of the most prominent cafes of the time, where the prince had his first experience imbibing a mint julep. He loved the cocktail so much that he wanted to stay for another. However, the reporters were concerned about returning to their stations before they were suspected of kidnapping royalty. But they were too late. By the time they arrived back at the prince's reception room, the Duke of Newcastle had already discovered the prince's absence, and he was furious. He threatened to have Thomson and Williams escorted from the building and to refuse further access to reports on the royal party. While the journalists did not protest, they did note that the prince's escapades would make a fascinating tale for their readers and suggested that the duke would become known as a negligent chaperone for allowing the "kidnapping" of the prince. Consequently, the duke changed his mind and allowed Thomson and Williams to remain and follow the royal party for the rest of its journey through the country.

George Foster Williams, Thomson's co-conspirator in these escapades, was another Pfaffian. He began his career as a journalist for the *New York*

Times but then left New York to work as a war correspondent, writing about Sheridan's military operations. General Grant liked the piece so much he invited the author to dine with him.

Another fan of Pfaff's, a male friend who seems to have admired and idealized Thomson, was the illustrator Thomas Nast. Born in Germany, Nast moved with his family to New York as a boy in 1846. Over the course of Nast's career, he became known as the "Father of the American cartoon." Like Thomson, Nast was interested in exposing corruption in the city. His depictions of the crooked Tammany Hall political machine and its ringleader William M. "Boss" Tweed were instrumental in bringing them down. Much of the working class of the era could not read, but they understood drawings, and the outrage of the general populace was ignited by Nast's illustrations. Nast is also credited with creating the modern version of Santa Claus and the political symbol of the elephant for the Republican Party.

When Thomson met Nast, the latter was the sixteen-year-old apprentice of Sol Eytinge at Frank Leslie's office, known in its infancy for its wood engravings. Many illustrators such as Nast and Eytinge would get their start there. Later, along with illustrations, the weekly would print daguerreotypes and then more advanced forms of photography until it folded in 1922. In Thomson's era, it would print sixteen sheets filled with stories, both fiction, such as the latest Charles Dickens short story, and nonfiction, such the description of the burning of P. T. Barnum's lavish Connecticut mansion, Iranistan, as well as poetry.

At Frank Leslie's office, Nast was both lovingly and patronizingly referred to as "Little Nast" in the diaries of his fellow illustrator Thomas Butler Gunn.[5] Nast would later accompany Thomson to Canada in 1858 to cover the legendary fight between the boxers John Heenan and John Morrissey.

Thomson began writing for *Frank Leslie's Illustrated Weekly* in 1856. At the time, the building was located on Frankfort Street, between William and Nassau. Thomson would have been able to wave from the window at his coworkers in the *Tribune* building. The front of the Leslie office was for the writers and illustrators and was likely where Thomson and Nast would conduct their work. The back of the office housed the printing presses and editorial offices.

Nast initially adored Thomson. In 1859, he attended a lecture of Thomson's, and Gunn wrote in his diary that Nast would "sit open mouthed, swallowing all Mort's teachings as gospel and resolving to act upon them."[6] Nast would later portray Thomson delivering his "Pluck" lecture to illustrious audiences at the Cooper Institute in New York. The lecture circuit was the best way for a writer to make money in the days before copyright laws, and Thomson would also give this lecture between 1859 and 1861 at other esteemed venues, such as the Irving Literary Institute in Philadelphia, the Young Men's Association of Chicago, and Village Hall in Montpelier, Vermont. The lives of Thomson and Nast became further entwined when Nast married Sarah Edwards in 1861. Edwards was the cousin of James Parton, who became Thomson's father-in-law in the same year.

In 1862, according to Gunn, Nast and Thomson had a slight falling out. Thomson had disliked a caricature drawn by Nast of Thomson's mother-in-law, Fanny Fern. Gunn had stated it was "not at all a good one and only recognizable from the little curls and hair-tendrils with which she surrounds her raddled old face."[7] Thomson confronted Nast and threatened him with personal vengeance if he published the caricature of Fern. Nast acted in a cool manner, causing Thomson to slink away to his father, Edwin, who was lurking in the background with a big stick.

It seems the two did not reconcile after that, and Nast would have as sad an ending as Thomson. In 1902, through his connection with President Theodore Roosevelt, who admired his work, Nast secured an appointment as the United States' Consul General to Guayaquil, Ecuador. Nast traveled to Guayaquil on July 1, 1902. Shortly after his arrival, there was an outbreak of yellow fever in the city, during which Nast caught the virus and succumbed to it on December 7, 1902. His body was brought back to the United States, and he was buried in the distinguished cemetery Woodlawn, among the graves of the wealthy. Nast's grave, however, is humble, secluded, and hard to find.

At *Frank Leslie's Illustrated Weekly*, Thomson also befriended Nast's famed mentor, Sol Eytinge, another frequenter of Pfaff's. At the height of his career, Eytinge was most famous for illustrating the US editions of Charles Dickens's books in 1867, when Dickens was due to tour the United States. Most famously, Eytinge illustrated *A Christmas Carol*. He included the scene in which Bob Cratchit carried Tiny Tim on his shoulders, the first time any illustrator had depicted that episode in a Charles Dickens publication. Eytinge also illustrated *Bleak House*, *Dombey and Son*, and *A Tale of Two Cities*. He illustrated for the authors Louisa May Alcott, Lord Alfred Tennyson, Edgar Allan Poe, Robert Browning, Oliver Wendell Holmes, and many others, as well.

Eytinge was born in 1833, and when he was twenty-three, he became an established staff artist for *Frank Leslie's Illustrated Weekly*. Gunn described Eytinge as "a handsome fellow, with a bold aquiline nose, and bright brown hair, tall withal, and prone to dress well. He has great talent with his pencil, but is over addicted to loafing, and has fits of blues. I think him a sensitive and kind-hearted fellow and his humors and queer speeches are infinitely amusing."[8]

In 1856, a scandal broke out, as Gunn reported that Eytinge was keeping a woman called Allie Vernon as his mistress. Vernon was mostly an author of children's stories. Her real name was Margaret (Winship) Wyckoff, and she wrote under the pseudonyms Allie Vernon, Margaret Winship Eytinge, Madge Elliot, and Bell Thorne. Gunn eagerly reported on various dramas in his diary, describing Vernon's husband showing up crying at a newspaper office where Eytinge worked and demanding the address of Eytinge's mother. The saga continued with Allie moving about the city, being squirreled away in secret to Brooklyn hotels away from her husband, who would then show up to demand access to his wife. A couple of weeks later, Gunn recorded that Allie was living with Eytinge in Brooklyn, where he had recently taken a little house.

At that point, Thomson was living in Brooklyn at 10 Hoyt Street with his wife, Anna, and, thinking Allie was "Mrs. Eytinge," invited her and her sister for dinner. He was later informed by a mutual friend that that was not the case. He went home to tell his wife, who became mortified; she had previously called upon Allie, believing the situation respectable. The impropriety had so upset her that she "cried for an hour about it on his [Thomson's] shoulder."[9] This is telling of the pressure on a white woman to maintain the appearance of respectability at every waking moment.

Eytinge was serious about his relationship with Allie, though. In Brooklyn in 1858, he married her. She already had two children from a previous marriage, one of whom took the name of her stepfather. She later became a world-renowned actress, Pearl Eytinge. Thomson was present at the wedding as groomsman, and the Reverend Henry Ward Beecher performed the marriage service. If the name Beecher seems familiar, it is because it held major significance at the time. Beecher was the brother of Harriet Beecher Stowe, the author of *Uncle Tom's Cabin*, an antislavery novel published in 1852. It was the best-selling novel of the nineteenth century and the second best-selling book that century, following the Bible. Though it is now criticized for stereotyping Black people, mainly because of how the characters were depicted in theatrical adaptations, the novel was influential enough at the time that it was said to lay the groundwork for the Civil War.

Henry Ward Beecher arrived at Plymouth Church in Brooklyn Heights in 1847 when he was in his mid-thirties. Well known for his abolitionist sentiments, Beecher drew crowds of Manhattanites to his Sunday sermons.

They crammed into aptly named "Beecher Boats," venturing across the East River to the city of Brooklyn to hear the mighty polemist speak. He often held mock auctions, shocking his audience into an understanding of the terrors of slavery. One of the most memorable auctions took place on Sunday, February 5, 1860. Nine-year-old Sally Maria Diggs, also known as "Pinky" because of her pale complexion, was placed on the auction block. The audience was scandalized to see a girl so young, and so white in complexion, offered for sale. A collection of nine hundred dollars was raised that day so that Pinky could be bought from her owner. Someone had placed a gold ring in the collection plate, which Beecher had plucked out and placed on the young girl's wedding finger. He is supposed to have said, "With this ring, I wed thee to freedom." Beecher also performed regular wedding ceremonies, such as that of Eytinge and Allie, and he would later do the same for Thomson.

Even once they were married men, Eytinge and Thomson continued to carouse together. On September 17, 1858, Thomson was seen drunk at the opera with Eytinge. Thomson had apparently gone to the *Tribune* office, had a friendly boxing match with Eytinge in the street, ridden uptown with him to the opera, and became drunk. On October 20, 1858, Gunn reported that Eytinge wanted to sketch the fight between the famed boxers John C. Heenan and John Morrissey but had demanded too much money, so, as mentioned earlier, Thomas Nast, his apprentice, was sent instead, along with Thomson.

In 1859, Gunn noted a couple more drunken tussles involving Thomson and Eytinge. In one instance, they had become intoxicated together, turning into "rowdies," and had confronted an acquaintance together regarding his defaming of Allie. In another instance at the *Tribune* office, an acquaintance had confronted Thomson over his "nasty piece" regarding an actor he had described as an "insane jackass, with his mane over his eyes."[10] Another drunken fisticuff had ensued.

In 1860, Eytinge began contributing to *Every Saturday* and *Harper's Weekly*. His relationship with Thomson seems to have fizzled out once they were no longer working together, as there are no accounts of the two men ever being seen together again.

Charles Pfaff died in 1890. He was remembered in the *Brooklyn Daily Eagle* as the proprietor of Pfaff's, and the article listed the men of note who had frequented the establishment, including the humorist Artemus Ward, Walt Whitman, and Mortimer Thomson. It was also noted that Charles Pfaff had outlived most of the men who frequented Pfaff's, including Thomson.

The original Pfaff's building is now at 643 Broadway, below Han's Deli.

It is a typical New York delicatessen, but if one descends into the basement, one can almost hear emanating from its exposed brick walls the voices of the artists who enjoyed their time there—and who, at some point during their lives, would be fated for the ill luck Madame Clifton might predict for them.

While at Madame Clifton's (a fifteen-minute walk east from Pfaff's), Thomson had observed accoutrements from the Golden Bell perfumery. In response to the Doesticks article regarding Madame Clifton and her abode, just like Mrs. E. Robinson, mentioned in Chapter 1, a reader became alarmed and offended by insinuations made by Doesticks. He wrote the following letter to the *New-York Tribune* on March 2, 1857:

> First, I am not nor never was, as is generally supposed, the proprietor of the establishment known as "The Golden Bell". . . .
>
> Secondly, in order to clear away the fog into which your reporter seems so unfortunately to have become enveloped, I will further state that immediately upon reading the article alluded to, I paid a visit to No. 185 Orchard street, to ascertain, if possible, who Madame Clifton was, and also to ascertain about the mysterious sign located in the corner of the parlor; also the unaccountable lot of Golden Bell Perfumery in the glass case up-stairs. To my utter astonishment, this gifted lady proved to be a Broadway fancy-shopkeeper, whose husband about one year ago purchased from the proprietor of the Golden Bell a bill of $300 or $400 worth of perfumery—the signboard included. Upon declining business, the balance of stock unsold has undoubtedly been removed to their present habitation. Deeming this explanation of the manner in which this Madame Clifton became possessed of these articles will be satisfactory to my numerous friends and relieve their anxious minds from any unpleasant misgivings, and believing also that your reporter, on his next visit, will have a better time generally, I remain, most respectfully, Yours & e., Marvin J. Merchant.[11]

Thomson's publishers must have taken note of this article: All references to the Golden Bell and its former proprietor were struck from Madame Clifton's chapter when the book was released the next year. In addition, all available versions of that newspaper edition seem to have scratched out the name of Marvin J. Merchant. This is what the original newspaper item had to say:

> One curious article, for a parlor ornament, stood in the corner of the room; it was the huge sign board of a perfumery store, and bore in large letters the name of [XXX] proprietor of the "Golden Bell," and the outline of a golden bell was also blazoned thereon in all the finery of Dutch metal and bronze. . . .
>
> What was the propriety of so very many bottles filled with perfumes and medicine did not at first appear, but the assortment of imprisoned odors, and liquid drugs, and the sign of the Golden Bell down stairs, and Madame Clifton, and the store of the Golden Bell in Broadway, and the proprietor thereof, so tangled themselves together in the brain of the reporter than he has never since that time been able to disconnect one from the other.[12]

Given Thomson's experience as a jewelry store clerk, it doesn't seem to have been that much of a stretch for his imagination to conclude that the perfume may have been inventory purchased from a store going out of business or that Madame Clifton may have been running multiple side hustles with her husband, but for the purposes of Thomson's article, he was only interested in inventing stories that might cast aspersions upon Madame Clifton's character.

Naturally, Marvin J. Merchant was concerned by the article's insinuation that Madame Clifton was running a house of ill repute. Prostitution provided a far higher income for women than the pittance paid by more "respectable" professions, such as seamstress, washerwoman, dressmaker, embroiderer, artificial flower maker, hot corn seller, and so forth. Prostitution could be found throughout the city at the time, with the main artery of business in what is now called SoHo, near where Pfaff's was located. *The Gentleman's Directory*, a guide to the brothels of New York City published in 1870, stated, "In passing up Broadway, any evening, between the hours of 7 and 11 o'clock, one is surprised to see so many well-dressed and comely females whose ages range from fifteen to twenty-five years, unattended by companions of the other sex."[13] In that era, any woman walking the streets alone was automatically presumed to be a prostitute.

In 1855, a chief resident physician on Blackwell's Island, Doctor William Sanger, interviewed two thousand women and published *The History of Prostitution* in 1858. The population of the city in 1860 was 813,669, and Sanger estimated the total number of prostitutes in Manhattan to be

7,860. He noted that some of these prostitutes were children. Some he interviewed confessed that they preferred prostitution to drunken abuse from husbands or the miserly pay and treatment of a servant. One can imagine those who made money through fortune telling felt similarly.

What was deeply hypocritical about attitudes toward prostitution at the time was that upper- and middle-class men were absolved from any blame for visiting houses of ill repute. Walt Whitman wrote that the "best classes of men" visited brothels, and men were allowed to keep their reputation while women were ruined for earning money from (or, like some of Doesticks's fortune tellers, even being indirectly associated with) one of the few kinds of work available to women that paid well. This morality regarding the kinds of work appropriate for women extended to fortune telling.

The first traceable record of Madame Clifton's clairvoyant services in the newspapers appeared on March 12, 1852, in the *New York Daily Herald*. She described herself as a "wonder of the world" and in an attention-grabbing headline offered a thousand-dollar reward to anyone who could match her ability at giving clients information regarding their health, wealth, marriage, and absent friends. She also bragged that she had been visited by over two thousand of the most respectable ladies in the city. This is likely a wild exaggeration. If she were that good, surely, would she not have enough customers via word of mouth and not have to advertise? Just as Thomson was an unreliable narrator, Madame Clifton's notice was loaded with hyperbole and promises that she doubtfully ever kept.

Besides offering business and legal advice, Madame Clifton's advertisements often offered cures for myriad diseases, including rheumatism in its worst stages, piles, liver complaint, disease of the kidneys, heart disease, affection of the lungs, and all other weaknesses to which a human is subjected. Why would such a woman be trusted? Both desperation and lack of financial resources were likely at the heart of it. Before the founding of the New York Academy of Medicine in 1847, "Traditional methods of medical practice were often more traumatic than the diseases themselves; avoidable infections were taking a powerful toll on lives in the best hospitals, and one in three women were dying in childbirth. Community health conditions were appalling, with 50 percent of children dying before the age of one."[14]

In other words, doctors had not earned the trust of the working or middle classes. Consider that this was an era when many doctors still believed in the practice of phrenology (the measurement of bumps on the skull to predict mental traits) and miasma theory (the theory that diseases such as cholera were caused by a noxious form of bad air). It is little wonder that the poor would seek advice from a cheaper variety of quack.

Madame Clifton's last New York advertisement for some years appeared in the summer of 1857, shortly after the release of the Doesticks article. Several months later she moved from 185 Orchard Street to 25 Orchard Street. However, between 1858 and 1861 she was mainly plying her trade at numerous locations in the South, including Memphis and New Orleans (where she wrote in November 1858 that she had "just arrived from Europe"), as well as Charleston, South Carolina; Augusta, Georgia; Macon, Georgia; and Natchez, Mississippi.

Starting on January 5, 1861, a flurry of advertisements appeared in the *Memphis Daily Argus* for most of the month of January and then early February. These announcements were for the services of an astrologist and doctress called Madame Arabella Clifton. In New York, the one official documentation of Madame Clifton appeared in the 1857–1858 *New York City Directory*, when "Amanda Clifton" was listed at 185 Orchard Street. Given the timing and the types of services advertised, it seems highly likely "Arabella Clifton" and "Amanda Clifton" are the same person. This Madame Clifton would also prescribe medicines for "all curable diseases."

On February 4, 1861, an article in the *Courier-Journal* reported that Madame Clifton had been arrested in Memphis for performing an abortion on a white woman. The main witness, Mrs. Banks, had been in Madame Clifton's employ and observed her performing the procedure through a keyhole. Madame Clifton was sent to jail for trial in default of a thousand dollars' bail. One does have to wonder if Madame Clifton's promise to prescribe medicines for all curable diseases also included abortion pills, powders, and pessaries, as the language for advertising abortion services in that era was often coded in such a way. Thomson had been so obsessed with exposing Madame Clifton for prostitution that he may have missed out on her other side gig.

One of the few decently paying professions for women was as a specialist in "women's health"—also a profession considered criminal in the nineteenth century. Among the most notorious of such specialists, and someone to whom Doesticks alludes in his Mrs. Hayes chapter (see Chapter 6), was Madame Restell. Her real name was Ann Trow Lohman, and she was an abortionist. Born in England, she began her career with an interest in midwifery and women's health, selling "female monthly pills" and "preventative powders," using carefully cloaked language in her newspaper advertisements. The law finally caught up with Madame Restell when she was begged and handsomely paid to perform a surgical abortion on Maria

Bodine, who she initially claimed was too far along in her pregnancy. Ms. Bodine fell ill after the abortion, and when she visited her regular physician, he demanded to know who had performed it. The doctor had Madame Restell arrested. She was put on trial and sentenced to one year in prison. Her fame spread, and she was deemed "The Wickedest Woman in New York" by the press, a sobriquet often accompanied by the accusation that she was a witch.

After Madame Restell finished her penitentiary sentence, she changed her practice, removing surgical abortions entirely, and focused on the sale of pills and powders. She also began taking note of the prominent businessmen and politicians whose mistresses visited her, using this information to prevent future arrests. Her business did so well that eventually she outbid the first Catholic archbishop of New York, the Most Reverend John Hughes, for land on Fifth Avenue, where she built her handsome mansion. She ran her business in the basement, almost directly opposite St. Patrick's Cathedral. This was a deliberate thumbing of her nose at the Catholic Church. Eventually, the postmaster inspector and moral reformist Anthony Comstock had her arrested. She was released on bail, but shortly afterward her maid found her dead in the bathtub, having committed suicide by slitting her throat.

The fact that Madame Clifton was associated with such a profession as abortion was enough to blacken her name, but the papers were not done smearing her. In March that year, another article associated Madame Clifton with a local, petty criminal named Bridget Tiernay, described as "a strapping Irish lass of some two hundred pounds weight [who] has a passionate fondness of the society of Madame Clifton."[15] Tiernay had recently been sent to jail after she was accused of entering the residence of a Minnie Savalle and stealing two pillow slips, a set of furs, and gold buttons. Just six days earlier, the same newspaper had written that she had been arrested for stealing silk dresses. It was also mentioned that after being released for that arrest she celebrated by becoming inebriated and had been rearrested for drunken behavior. On August 28, 1861, the *Memphis Daily Appeal* stated that she had been found guilty of larceny and had been sentenced to three years in the penitentiary.

On March 13, 1861, Madame Clifton's release from a six-week sentence in jail was announced in the *Memphis Daily Argus*. Madame Clifton had then issued a warrant for the arrest of her former employee, Mrs. Banks, on the charge of perjury. Mrs. Banks was the person who provided evidence in court that had ultimately led to Madame Clifton's jail sentence.

A pitiful article appealing for Madame Clifton's cause later appeared in the *Argus* newspaper on March 26 of that year. It claimed the charges against Madame Clifton were "wholly unsubstantiated" and that Madame Clifton was a lonely widow, engaged in the simple trade of fortune telling, which was "old as society." Moreover, Madame Clifton had been treated with extreme prejudice since the terrible charges laid against her. She had been "exiled from a half-dozen houses, though promptly paying her bills and injuring none."[16] Four days later, a similar but shorter article also appeared in the *Courier-Journal* in Louisville, Kentucky. It is possible these were advertisements masquerading as articles placed by Madame Clifton, or perhaps they were written by a sympathetic reporter or a reporter who was being bribed, having procured Madame Clifton's more illicit services in the past.

Madame Clifton disappeared from the news for about nine years following these sad claims. She reappeared in the *New York Daily Herald* on April 28, 1870, when it was announced she was then living at 176 Bleecker Street, just a few blocks away from Pfaff's. She was still promising to cure all diseases in their worst form. A final article promising the same appeared in the *New York Herald* on July 26, 1871. Shortly afterward, she likely succumbed to one of the diseases she promised to cure.

Chapter 3

Madame Prewster

Lenormand Card: Heart (Meaning = *Love*)

Doesticks's walk to see Madame Prewster, the most "dangerous" of all the witches, seemed otherworldly.[1] "The driving drops had nearly drowned the sunshine, and through the sickly light that still survived, everything looked dim and spectral," he wrote, ominously. "Unearthly cars, drawn by ghostly horses, glided swiftly through the mist, the intangible apparitions which occupied the drivers' usual stands hailing passengers with hollow voices, and proffering, with impish finger and goblin wink, silent invitations to ride."[2]

Doesticks divulged his knowledge of Madame Prewster's history with glee. She had been active as a fortune teller before any of the other witches, and she had been known to the police for about fourteen years. If her evil doings were published and justice served, Doesticks pondered, surely Madame Prewster would spend a lengthy sentence in the penitentiary. He was perhaps referring to the penitentiary on Blackwell's Island, reserved for the criminals who committed what were considered the most heinous crimes of the day, including murder, theft, and abortion. One might envision a character like Fredericka "Marm" Mandelbaum, a New York City entrepreneur who operated as a criminal fence to street gangs and crooks in the Five Points neighborhood. It is believed that over her "career," which likely ran between 1862 and 1884, she handled millions of dollars' worth of stolen goods.

Doesticks claimed he traveled by foot to see Madame Prewster as he could not stand to stew for an hour in a steaming car or spend time on a leaky omnibus. Instead, he toughed it out in the rain, wearing a huge pair of waterproof boots and a felt hat that he said shed water like a duck. Avoiding being hit by umbrellas and curious pedestrians, who were likely puzzled by his choice of attire in the pouring rain, he finally arrived at the domicile of Madame Prewster at 373 Bowery.

Madame Prewster's advertisements made numerous inflated promises, offering to answer all questions in astrology, love, and law matters, noting that she consulted books and oracles relied upon by Napoleon. Clearly appealing to the ladies, she further assured seekers that she would tell the name of their future husbands.

Doesticks's knock was answered by a "greasy girl" who admitted the damp and dripping visitor. She was apparently so alarmed by his appearance that she took a defensive stance, with fists at the ready. Doesticks immediately mentioned astrology and the servant let her guard down. If Doesticks wanted to see Madame Prewster, the fee was a dollar and a half, up front. Having paid the requisite money, he was escorted to a reception room, an uncarpeted apartment of six by eight feet with six chairs, an unlit stove, a feeble table, one spittoon, and two coal scuttles. Through the window, he observed wandering cats, clotheslines, chimneys, the low roofs of stables, oil-mills, a Peck Slip ferryboat, bone-boiling establishments, and a soap and candle manufacturer. The air was perfumed with a "greasy fragrance," he scoffed.

Doesticks waited for an hour and a half, silently grumbling all the while that he would march out but for the "warlike servant." Finally, he was brought in to see Madame Prewster in the kitchen. She was clearly a mother or grandmother: Doesticks made mention of a "feeble child," a toddler who was seated on top of a dinner pot, with one foot in a saucepan and pounding on a washer boiler as though it were a drum. The impoverished child became engaged with sprinkling bits of charcoal and the splinters of a broom on unbaked bread.

Madame Prewster seemed unfazed by this. She was seated in a Windsor rocking chair and wore a brightly colored shawl. By Doesticks's assertion, she could be any age from forty-five to 120 (according to newspapers, Madame Prewster was thirty-nine when Doesticks visited her). Doesticks noted, "Her face is so oily that wrinkles won't stay in it. . . . Grim, grizzled, and stony-eyed, is this juicy old Sibyl."[3] Madame Prewster seemed to have recently rolled out of bed, he thought, even though it was just past noon, and she yawned a lot, spending much time gazing at Doesticks before giving him cards to shuffle.

Doesticks had seen a lot of trouble, she told him, some of it in business, some in love, but there were brighter days in store, especially once he married. He would marry a light-haired woman, who would have dealings with a "dark complexioned" man, which would be bad for Doesticks. His first wife would have four letters in her name, which seems to be the first time in the book one of the clairvoyants made a vaguely accurate prediction. But then, disappointingly, Madame Prewster rattled through a series of names. Emma? Anna? Ella? Jane? Etta? Lucy? Cora? Landing on Mary, Doesticks let that be the name of his true love. Mary, according to Madame Prewster, was a good girl. She was far away right now, but soon she would be close, and they would marry. Then it was Madame Prewster's turn to guess Doesticks's name. It began with "M," he told her, and contained eight letters. She went through every male name beginning with M from Mark to Melchisedek before giving up, which is a wonder: Mortimer was a common name in the 1850s.

Madame Prewster forged ahead, inviting her client to make three wishes on the cards, and she would tell him if he they would be granted or not. He wished to be rich, to marry the light-haired maiden, and to "smash the dark-complexioned man."[4] Happily, Madame Prewster predicted that all his wishes would come true. Then, perhaps as a concession for her earlier blunders, she suggested that he could make one secret wish. He wished for an enormous amount of ready money and was told his secret wish would be granted. Answering Doesticks's further inquiries, she told him he would have one wife and four children.

At this point, Madame Prewster began to wriggle uneasily, and deciding he "respected her 'rheumatics' "[5] Doesticks took his leave, before noting to himself that even though it would take the reader a mere five minutes to read about this experience, the whole process had taken forty-five minutes because Madame Prewster was so slow. As the servant was seeing him out, he observed that she had a rolling pin under her apron, ready to use in case he became boisterous.

Thomson was cruel in allowing Madame Prewster to continue past the name Anna: He had been courting a young woman by the name of Anna Van Cleve for several years at the time of his visit. According to Thomas Butler Gunn, they had known each other since "childhood," though not since Thomson's childhood, as there was a nine-year difference between them. In 1854, when Thomson was first moving to Brooklyn with his family

and friend Ed Wells, in his correspondence with Van Cleve, who would
have been thirteen, he was already calling her "his wife" and affirming his
intentions to marry her to her parents. Van Cleve, in turn, was corresponding affectionately with Thomson and his family. Van Cleve's parents seem
to have expressed some concern regarding their daughter's youth, but they
also had a loving and longstanding relationship with Thomson. Following
three years of waiting and Thomson setting himself up financially, Van
Cleve visited for several months in 1856, and then they married.

Van Cleve was born on December 20, 1840, in Cincinnati, Ohio, but her
family is famous for its association with Minnesota, and their Minneapolis
home is now listed on the National Register of Historic Places. Her father
was Horatio Phillips Van Cleve. He was born in Lawrenceville, New Jersey,
attended Princeton University, and graduated from the West Point Military Academy before joining the United States Fifth Infantry Regiment as
a Second Lieutenant, where he stayed for five years, until 1836.

Van Cleve's mother, Charlotte Ouisconsin Clark, was born in Wisconsin
but shortly after birth moved with her father's regiment to Fort Snelling,
Minnesota, where the family resided for many years, until she married
Horatio in 1836. For the next twenty years of their marriage they lived
in Ohio, Missouri, and Michigan, finally returning to Minnesota in 1856.
Charlotte is most notable for being active in the suffragette movement but
also for her numerous books and articles, particularly documenting Minnesota history, with her personal observations being a part of the narrative.

The marriage of Anna and Mortimer took place in 1857, the same year
the "Witches of New York" articles were being published in the *New-York
Tribune*. Shortly following Thomson's visits to various tenements—and it
should be noted that two of the fortune tellers he visited had the telltale
pockmarks from the disease—Thomson came down with smallpox. A vi-
ral infection that left the skin of the victim covered in unsightly blister-
filled pustules, smallpox could lead to arthritis, deformity, and, of course,
death. Smallpox was highly contagious, so it was important for those who
caught it to go into quarantine. In 1856, the Smallpox Hospital opened on
Blackwell's Island. Anyone, rich or poor, who had contracted smallpox was
supposed to go into quarantine in the hospital. The first and second floors
were open spaces reserved for the poor, and the third floor was reserved
for those who could pay for private rooms.

Alas, records for the Smallpox Hospital are not available, so there is no
way of verifying whether Thomson quarantined there or not. It is also a
possibility that Thomson decided to convalesce at home in Brooklyn after contracting smallpox. It is certain he recovered. A photograph reveals

the scarring that signified recovery from smallpox, marks that would have shown on his face at the time of his wedding.

On October 24, 1857, a characteristic Doesticks tongue-in-cheek item appeared in the *New Haven Palladium*, describing an "irruption into this city of long bearded men, from New York,"[6] followed by the announcement that Thomson had married Miss Anna H. Van Cleve, of Minnesota, in New Haven, at the home of her uncle, Professor J. W. Gibbs of Yale College, by the Reverend Dr. Van Cleve of Minnesota. Following the wedding, she moved into Thomson's Brooklyn residence with Thomson's parents and Ed Wells. She was often fondly referred to by loved ones and acquaintances as "Nannie" or "Chips."

On November 15, 1857, Gunn described his first meeting with Thomson's bride. He was smitten right away. "Doesticks household a pleasant one. His mother, wife and a friend who resides with them. Doesticks wife has a very pretty, innocent face, kind eyes, and soft dark hair. She is quite young, says not much, and evidently thinks him the cleverest fellow in the world."[7] Gunn continued to write of Van Cleve's innocence and youth in other entries, which contrasted greatly with how Thomson would write about the witches. Van Cleve fell into the approved role of the "good wife." In the coming months, Gunn continued to reveal more particulars of the marriage.

> Sat talking for a hour and a half with the two Mrs Thomsons and an-other lady, there present. Doesticks wife looking as pretty, and good, and innocent as ever. Was shown a series of daguerrotypes [*sic*] of her, from the age of five and upwards he & Thomson appearing, also, in most of them. Ah! happy Doesticks! married to the girl he loves and prosperous. And, I believe, thoroughly deserving his happiness.[8]

Things were looking up for Thomson not just in love but also in his career. He was writing for reputable newspapers and periodicals, the *New-York Tribune* and *Frank Leslie's Illustrated Weekly* among them. He also briefly co-owned the *New York Picayune*. His books were being published and reviewed. He was also hanging out with *the* literary movers and shakers of the time, among them the newspaper columnist Fanny Fern and the biographer James Parton, and he was living in the stylish Brooklyn neighborhood of Fort Greene.

At the time, Fort Greene was an up-and-coming area, with recently built, handsome townhouses, tree-lined streets, and the new Washington Park for family strolls; the neighborhood was second only in prestige to the wealthier Brooklyn Heights. The prosperous residents lived practically side by side with recently arrived Irish immigrants who had escaped the Irish potato famine. An enclave of unoccupied territory that extended from Flushing Avenue southward to DeKalb Avenue and bounded by Classon Avenue on the east and Ryerson Street (where Walt Whitman lived from May 1855 to May 1856) on the west become known as "Young Dublin," and the New York Times reported on the alarming poverty of this shanty-town. The place was populated by dogs, pigs, hens, and even the odd goat. The valley was low and wet, and nine out of ten shanties were reported to have only one room of an average of twelve square feet to serve an entire family. The shanties were meanly furnished with a soapbox, a bed, table, and perhaps a few chairs or benches. This poverty is similar to that found in some of the homes Thomson witnessed while visiting his witches and would have contrasted with Thomson's household, which could afford servants and privacy for the family members.

Thomson would have traveled between his Brooklyn home and his Manhattan newspaper offices with ease because stagecoach lines ran along nearby Myrtle Avenue and Fulton Street, to whisk Brooklyn residents to the Fulton Ferry. From the Manhattan pier to Printing House Square, it was a ten-minute walk.

On December 25, 1857, a delightful description of Christmas jovialities appeared in Gunn's diaries. His presents, gifted by a friend, which he had opened in the morning, included a silver pen and pencil case, gold pen, and neckerchief, all appropriate goodies for an illustrator. While out visiting and running errands, he dropped off a note to Thomson from James Parton. He described Thomson meeting him in a gorgeous red dressing gown and urging Gunn to join his family for Christmas revelry.

New Year's Day in antebellum New York was a day to go calling on one's friends, acquaintances, and neighbors. It was called "first footing," and Gunn describes sharing this ritual with Thomson, who was reluctant to go out, enjoying his newfound domestic coziness. Van Cleve, however, was a more complex lady than Gunn first gave her credit for. She befriended Fanny Fern's daughter, Grace Eldredge, who was about the same age.[9] It would have been a fifteen-minute walk for the Thomsons from their Brooklyn home on Hoyt Street to Grace's home at 33 Oxford Street in Fort Greene. On January 5, 1858, Gunn described visiting the Thomsons for dinner and said the feature of the night was Thomson's new bride appearing in male attire. Perhaps encouraged by Grace Eldredge and her mother, who, it seemed, liked to go out on the town dressed as men, Van Cleve developed a taste for cross-dressing, and she appeared at dinner in her husband's clothing. Gunn described her as looking "exceedingly pretty" dressed this way. Doesticks wasn't the only one to try dressing as the opposite sex.

On March 18, 1858, Doesticks published a mocking article on married life in the *San Francisco Daily Evening Bulletin* titled "How Philander Doesticks Became a Broken-In Husband." According to the newly married Doesticks, all his wife had to do to break up his bachelor habits (whatever they were) was to give him the incorrect item he had requested. Say Mr. Doesticks asked for milk, Mrs. Doesticks would get pepper, and when Mr. Doesticks wanted bread, he would receive hot water, to the point that Mr. Doesticks had to start fetching domestic items all for his own poor, weary self. He further noted, "I am thoroughly convinced that a woman with plenty of ready-made tears can tame the most obdurate man simply with this aqueous ammunition."[10] By the admission of Mr. Doesticks, he had been convinced to buy dresses, bonnets, and fur capes (every-day middle-class clothing for women), all on the strength of the tears of Mrs. Doesticks.

At another party that year on February 24, 1858, Gunn declared in his diary that Van Cleve was "the prettiest woman there; with her silky dark hair worn smoothly and plainly, her kind eyes, innocent voice and sweet, pleasant laugh."[11] All this loveliness would take a dark turn. In September of that year, Gunn reported visiting Van Cleve, who had been in bed for "some weeks," sick and pregnant. Gunn noted that Van Cleve had probably become a wife too young.

Childbirth was fraught with risk at this time. In the early part of the nineteenth century, the typical American woman had between seven to eight live births in her lifetime. Birth control was frowned upon, provided by questionable doctors, and often dangerous, sometimes resulting in illness or death. Moreover, the infant mortality rate in 1850 per 1,000 children in the United States for white families was 216.8 and for Black families, 340. Not only were married (and sometimes unmarried) women destined to the possibility of frequent pregnancies; they were also burdened with the risk of dying in childbirth or giving birth to a stillborn.[12] These are challenges that would have faced both working-class women like the fortune tellers and middle-class women such as Van Cleve.

Van Cleve seemed to have made a brief recovery from her illness, but then on December 22, 1858, she died after giving birth to her and Thomson's first child. She had reached the age of eighteen just two days prior. Two days following, Gunn dedicated seven pages of his diary to her funeral service and burial, plus a keepsake verse from the service, in heartbreaking detail. He wrote that a relative instructed attendees not to try to offer condolences to Thomson, as he might break down: "The poor fellow, it seemed, was dreadfully cut up. Said Scranton, He put his arms round my neck and cried for half an hour, when I came."[13]

On Christmas Eve, 1858, when Gunn attended Anna's funeral, held at the family home at 102 Hampden Street in Brooklyn, he mentioned that a Mr. Storrs had conducted the service because Beecher was out of town. "Mort knows him very well."[14] Thomson had also sought consolation from Henry Ward Beecher. Thomson is likely to have come to know Beecher when he moved to Brooklyn in 1856. They moved in similar circles of bohemians and Brooklyn abolitionists, and Beecher knew Fanny Fern well: Fern attended the boarding school of his sister Catharine Beecher, and it is documented that they met several times.

Gunn wrote of Thomson at the funeral service: "The fellow's face was piteous to look upon[,] a fixed, contracted crying look and he shook perpetually, like a paralytic. Grasping his mother's hand as she sat, veiled in her deep mourning, he sat with his head thrown back, as though fixed to struggle with and endure his great grief. I only ventured to steal a glance or two at him, had I done more I should have cried too."[15]

Between attending the service and heading to the burial, Gunn pressed Fanny Fern for details of the death. The birth had initially appeared to be a successful and expedited one, and the doctor had been dismissed from the house while a happy family doted on the newborn and drank to the mother's and baby's health with liquor ("unwisely," as Gunn evaluated in his account). Some hours later, Van Cleve had been beset with convulsions. Fanny Fern, who lived nearby, was sent for around three or four in the morning so she could be with Van Cleve, while Thomson ran out to fetch a doctor, making stops at more than one doctor's home, as some refused to go to the house at such an early hour. When Fern arrived, a doctor was there, and Thomson was soaked from the rain, just as he had been when he visited Madame Prewster. Van Cleve was said to be suffering horribly. Fern nursed Van Cleve until she died and reported that the convulsions were so horrible that Van Cleve had bitten through her lips and tongue. Thomson was not present for her last moments. Gunn reported that Fern had said that "shortly after death the dead girls face looked heavenly."[16]

Following the service, the party headed to Green-Wood Cemetery to bury Van Cleve. Opened in 1838, it was the most famous cemetery in New York City at the time. Out of Thomson's earshot, more talk of Van Cleve's tragic death ensued among the party. Thomson would not see his newborn son, Mark, at that time, who was to be cared for the rest of his life primarily by grandmothers, both on Thomson's and Van Cleve's side. So much for the one wife and four children Madame Prewster had promised him.

One of the first ads for Madame Prewster appeared in 1847 in a Philadelphia newspaper: She was practicing at 968 Wood Street and offering to interpret dreams or tell people the name of their future wife or husband. She charged fifty cents for women and one dollar for gentlemen. Charging double for men was a policy she retained throughout her career.

How to account for the different charges? Thomson often insinuated in his narrative that fortune tellers were prostitutes in disguise and that the reason they would either not admit gentlemen or charge them double is because they did not want to run into former clients. If this was heavily on Thomson's mind, it must have been in other men's minds, too. However, from the perspective of a woman living in the mid-nineteenth century, fortune tellers were inviting people not just into their homes but sometimes, with living space being so tight, their bedrooms. This put the women in a vulnerable position. As women were viewed as the property of men in that era, and poor women especially were fair game, one can only imagine the level of attacks, sexual assault, and sexual harassment to which the women were susceptible.

In fact, working-class women were considered, by default, to be promiscuous. John Dixon Mann, who wrote an influential forensic textbook in the 1890s, said "women of the lower classes" were "accustomed to rough play with individuals both of their own and of the opposite sex" and had therefore "acquire[d] the habit of defending themselves against sportive violence."[17] Therefore, if a working-class woman was raped, it was deemed to be her own fault. Similarly, in 1815, Onesipherous W. Bartley wrote in *A Treatise on Forensic Medicine or Medical Jurisprudence* that female orgasm was not possible in rape and that conception "must depend on the exciting passion that predominates; to this effect, the *oestrum/veneris* must be excited to such a degree as to produce that mutual *orgasm* which is essentially necessary to impregnation; if any desponding or depressing passion presides, this will not be accomplished."[18]

Not only were women magically expected to prevent pregnancy in the case of rape, but were they attacked, they were considered to ultimately be the more responsible party. Take the words of Charles Loring Brace, who wrote: "There is no reality in the sentimental assertion that the sexual sins of the lad are as degrading as those of the girl. The instinct of the female is more toward the preservation of purity, and therefore her fall is deeper— an instinct grounded in the desire of preserving a stock, or even the necessity of perpetuating our race."[19] The scholar Christine Stansell also discussed the belief that a woman's morality was responsible for whether she was raped or not, offering the example of a case reported in the Court of General Sessions, *People v. Gunning et al.*, from December 13, 1858. A seamstress had taken six men to court for gang rape. During the trial, witnesses were brought forth, including a cousin, the cousin's friends, and respective wives, who gave unfavorable testimony to the victim's character, including her reputation in the old country.[20] Allowing a man into one's home, even one's bedroom, posed a physical risk to women's safety and reputation. It is little wonder that fortune tellers like Madame Prewster charged men more; they were more of a liability.

After leaving Philadelphia, Madame Prewster would move to the Lower East Side, keeping many addresses on or close to the Bowery. Movement among women who lived in Madame Prewster's neighborhood was common. Poverty often forced people to move from one space to the next when they couldn't pay rent. Further, there were not many who would have chosen to remain long in such a neighborhood, if possible. In 1857, the Bowery was known for its cheap entertainment. Close to the crime-ridden neighborhood of Five Points, the Bowery was littered with tattoo parlors, beer saloons, dime museums (they appeared later, in the 1880s), and black-eye specialists (if you got a black eye in a fight, there were specialists who would cover it with makeup). In the latter part of the nineteenth century, the Bowery would sprout the grisly McGurk's Suicide Hall, which was exactly what it sounded like. There a desperate person down on their luck could purchase a poisoned drink, then go to a discrete place to commit suicide.

P. T. Barnum, the impresario of dime museums, opera singers, and later the circus, started out on the Bowery in 1835 with the exhibition of Joice Heth, who it was claimed was George Washington's nanny, still alive at the age of 161. Of course, this was a hoax, as the pathologist pronounced her no older than eighty at the time of her death.

The conditions of the tenements on the Bowery and most of the Lower East Side were notoriously terrible, but unlike Thomson, who blamed this squalor on the impoverished people living in the buildings, other writers would place the responsibility at the feet of the rich. Fanny Fern, for example, wrote: "Alas! if some of the money spent on corporation-dinners, on Fourth of July fireworks, and on public balls, where rivers of champagne are worse than wasted, were laid aside for the cleanliness and purification of these terrible localities which slay more victims than the war is doing, and whom nobody thinks of numbering."[21] One can imagine Fanny Fern to be more sympathetic than Thomson to the plight of Madame Prewster; she expressed compassion about women living in the tenements in her novel *Ruth Hall*. As a woman who had experienced poverty and destitution at first hand, she wrote:

Opposite was one of those large brick tenements, let out by rapacious landlords, a room at a time at griping rents, to poor emigrants, and others, who were barely able to prolong their lease of life from day to day. At one window sat a tailor, with his legs crossed, and a torn straw hat perched awry upon his head, cutting and making coarse garments for the small clothing-store in the vicinity, whose Jewish owner reaped all the profits. At another, a pale-faced woman, with a handkerchief bound round her aching face, bent over a steaming wash-tub, while a girl of ten, staggering under the weight of a basket of damp clothes, was stringing them on lines across the room to dry. At the next window sat a decrepit old woman, feebly trying to soothe in her palsied arms the wailings of a poor sick child. And there, too, sat a young girl, from dawn till dark, scarcely lifting that pallid face and weary eyes—stitching and thinking, thinking and stitching. God help her![22]

It was likely this terrible poverty that caused women to turn to professions that danced on the margins of the law. Thomson was not greatly exaggerating Madame Prewster's reputation for arranging what would have been considered unsavory marriages at the time, and according to some news reports, Madame Prewster freely admitted her involvement in forming such matches, though according to her claims she had no idea the partnerships were to become "dishonorable."

In 1855, a mother of a "respectable" family wrote an open letter to Fernando Wood, New York's mayor, in the *Evansville Daily Journal*. The mother's story detailed how she had raised a family of eleven, all now married and "doing respectable business" except for her fifteen-year-old daughter. The previous summer, her daughter and a school friend had seen an advertisement in the *Herald* written by a man looking for a wife, and the daughter had answered the advertisement. She was told to meet a "Mrs. Prewster" by the corner of Great Jones Street and Bowery. For five dollars, which the daughter had obtained by selling earrings and a breast pin, Mrs.

Prewster detailed her vision of the girl's future husband. She also predicted an imminent spouse for her school friend. The girl had successfully met with a man and gone on a date with him to Coney Island, so the daughter was excited by the prospects offered by Mrs. Prewster. At Mrs. Prewster's home, the daughter met with a man who had dark eyes and told the girl he had dreamed of her. She was taken in by his flattery. They started meeting regularly at Mrs. Prewster's.

The mother claims to have had no suspicions that something was awry, as she had many married brothers and sisters her daughter could have been visiting at that time of night. "All at once I saw her shape alter and her lively spirits gone,"[23] the mother reported in her letter. The mother asked what was troubling her daughter, and she answered that her school friend had run away from home and was now living with a bad man in a bad house. The daughter began crying and confessed to her mother that she was in a "family way": She had been impregnated by a man who turned out to be already married, with four children. The mother found her daughter a boarding house on Lispenard Street and was assured by the lady of that house that she would be confined until she gave birth and the baby given away. With this story, the mother urged the mayor to shut down the fortune telling business, which had ruined the lives of two young women.

This dubious matchmaking practice of Madame Prewster's was further confirmed in a November 1855 article in the *New York Times*. A reporter visited Prewster at her abode, then at 76 Madison Street, near Chatham, a primarily European-Jewish neighborhood on the Lower East Side. On the second floor, the reporter and his friend were admitted by a little girl "in a ragged dress."[24] They saw Madame Prewster in her bedroom, where she was seated in a rocking chair, likely the same one she sat in while telling Doesticks his fortune. Like Thomson, this reporter used his description of the appearance of Madame Prewster as an immediate way of discrediting anything she might have to say: "I would be afraid to say how many chins were possessed by Madame Prewster. They lay one behind the other just like reserve battalions. . . . Madame Prewster was stout. If she had discovered the philosopher's stone, she had evidently changed it into a loaf of bread."[25]

After telling the reporter's friend his future, which the reporter rejected both to Madame Prewster's face and in various written asides, he questioned her about her practice of making marital matches. Madame Prewster bragged to him that she had made over three hundred suitable matches in the last year. She kept a list of female clients looking for male partners, then made introductions at her home. The reporter asked if she had ever made introductions that she was sure *wouldn't* result in marriage. Madame Prewster seemed scandalized at the suggestion.

It is possible, though, that Madame Prewster was invested in making genuine marriage matches. For example, on January 11, 1856, the *New York Daily Herald* announced a marriage had taken place at Madame Prewster's matrimony office on 76 Madison Street. Further, while it was claimed in some newspapers that the marriages and partnerships enabled by the introduction of such con artists as Madame Prewster led to unhealthy and ruinous homes, one can't help observing that even the so-called respectable marriages of the middle and upper classes produced their own form of misery. Through marriage, women of all classes lost all financial independence, leaving upper- and middle-class women just as vulnerable as those in the lower classes.

In the year Anna Van Cleve died, the police went on a fortune-teller-arresting spree. Among the psychics they called upon and arrested was Madame Prewster. Again, Madame Prewster freely confessed to her practice of matchmaking, cynically admitted her fortune telling vocation was a "humbug," and asserted, "The ticket swindlers and all others have had their turn, and she thought the fortune tellers might as well come in for a share of patronage."[26]

What is remarkable about Madame Prewster's arrest is not just her candor (there is, of course, the possibility that she was coerced or that the police reported her confession incorrectly) but also her argument that the ticket swindlers and "all others" had had their turn. Madame Prewster was correct in asserting that in the 1850s there were indeed many scammers in the city of varying kinds, from the runners who greeted newly arrived immigrants at Castle Clinton, to "humbugs" such as P. T. Barnum, to the corrupt politicians of Tammany Hall. Just over a decade before these arrests, a couple of doors down from Madame Prewster at 375 Bowery, a Dr. Taylor sold his Balsam of Liverwort for consumption and liver complaint. Ads by S. J. Hinsdale for the tonic boasted great success, to the point of advising readers they should be wary of purchasing any imitation tonics.[27]

One of the most corrupt institutions in the city was the police department itself. The year Thomson visited the fortune tellers and advocated for their arrests, 1857, was a tumultuous one for the New York police department. Republican Party reformers in the capital of Albany formed a new metropolitan police force and attempted to eradicate the municipal police. They passed a metropolitan police bill that would consolidate the police in New York, Brooklyn, Staten Island, and Westchester County. The mayor at the time, Fernando Wood, and his police force, the Municipals, resisted this change for several months, so two police forces operated in the city at the same time, and these two factions became hostile toward each other. The Municipals were formed largely of immigrants, and the Metropolitans were composed of those of Anglo-Dutch heritage, or Nativists, as they called themselves. With the divisions of the two forces in place, criminals began to play the police against each other, with one force arresting and the other force letting them go. The tension climaxed in mid-June 1857, when a Metropolitan police captain attempted to deliver a warrant for the mayor's arrest but was thrown out by a group of Municipals. The Metropolitans then marched to City Hall with a second warrant, only to be met by a group of Municipals and a crowd of toughs. Fisticuffs ensued. The Metropolitans, who were outnumbered, withdrew, but the next day they successfully served their warrant to Wood, with assistance from the New York State–controlled Seventh Regiment. Wood eventually conceded, and the Metropolitans gained control.

One of Madame Prewster's investigating officers, Sergeant Birney, was also going through some turbulence of his own. In the mid-1850s, he was involved in a series of investigations to clean up fraud and corruption in New York City. It was reported in the newspapers that Birney was prosecuting unlicensed liquor dealers, bogus lottery systems, and investigating counterfeit notes that were printed in New York City at the office of a Mister Harrison, at 82 Duane Street, as directed by Madam Zaifman (her name sounds like she could have been one of Doesticks's fortune tellers). However, Birney was dismissed from the force in March 1859 when it was found he too was guilty of corruption. Among the court reports, it was suggested that Birney was taking bribes, including cash and a diamond ring for his wife.

Another curious aspect of the article detailing the arrests of the fortune tellers is the mention of a Dr. Bland, who lived on the Lower East Side. When he was arrested in 1859 for running a bogus operation of manufacturing and selling love powders, he was called by the newspapers "[a] most amusing rogue" and a "precious operator" who was "living in elegance." In contrast, when reports of the female fortune tellers' arrests appeared in the newspapers, they were described as "evil," with words such as "humbug" and "witchcraft" abundant. As opposed to Dr. Bland's elegant quarters, those women were also said to be living in a "low rookery" and a "miserable, filthy looking abode."[28] Even as con artists, these women were mostly doomed to impoverished living.

It also appears that Dr. Bland did not have the additional pressure of being the caretaker of children. When Thomson visited Madame Prewster, he observed a "feeble child" sitting in the dinner pot, and in the 1855 report, the men were greeted by a "ragged child." There also seems to be no mention of a Mr. Prewster, so potentially Madame Prewster was the main breadwinner of the family. Women were always paid far less than men, often based on the assumption that there was a husband somewhere pulling in a higher salary. Most working-class women would make between fifty cents and two dollars a week in the 1850s. Consider that, in comparison, unskilled male laborers earned roughly seven dollars a week. Moreover, the women workers who lived in the tenements and worked these backbreaking jobs were also responsible for keeping their own house and hauling groceries, coal, firewood, and children up and down stairs. Working women struggled to afford lodging, candles, coal, and firewood. In turn their children regularly became ill with eyestrain, fatigue, malnutrition, pneumonia, and consumption (known today as tuberculosis). Other prevalent and life-threatening diseases in the tenements included yellow fever, smallpox, and cholera, as well as diarrhea (which was enough to allow Thomson to be sent home from serving in the Civil War).

Fanny Fern wrote not only of the horrifying conditions of the tenements but also the effects that living in such an environment must have on children: "There were slaughter-houses, with pools of blood in front, round which gambolled pigs and children; there were piles of garbage in the middle of the street, composed of cabbage dumps, onion-skins, potato-parings, old hats, and meat-bones, cemented with cinders, and penetrated by the sun's rays, emitting the most beastly odors. . . . How *can* those children ever get a chance to grow up anything but penitentiary inmates?"[29] In *The Dangerous Classes of New York*, Charles Loring Brace wrote of the prospects of poor tenement children: "Out of 452 criminal children received into the House of Refuge in New York during 1870, only 187 had both parents living, so that nearly sixty per cent had lost one or both of their parents, or were otherwise separated from them."[30]

One of the last records for Madame Prewster appears in the 1867–1868 *New York City Directory*, where she was listed as an astrologist and the widow of "Richard." What became of the child in the dinner pot is unknown.

Chapter 4

‖‖

Madame Widger

Lenormand Card: House (Meaning = *Home*)

Doesticks professed that he hoped Madame Widger would be a "blushing blooming maiden" but instead found her to be "an ancient dame, whose very wrinkles dated back to the eighteenth century."[1] Madame Widger was only forty-four years old when Doesticks encountered her in 1857. Not only was Doesticks disappointed by Madame Widger's looks, but he was further displeased by the appearance of her estate on First Avenue, a three-story brick house that "seemed to have that architectural disease which is a perpetual epidemic among the tenant-houses of the city, and which makes them look as if they had all been dipped in a strong solution of something that had taken the skin off."[2]

After Doesticks rang the bell multiple times, the door was finally answered by a man Doesticks called elderly (perhaps he was also in his forties), with "weak eyes." The man seemed as feeble as the "shabbily furnished room" with "treacherous chairs" to which Doesticks was guided to wait. The furniture included a cooking stove, an iron kettle, a trunk, a faded carpet, a rocking chair, and a table. A certificate of membership of the New York State Agricultural Society, given in Albany to Mr. M. G. Bivins, hung on the wall. It appeared to be a religious household because portraits of saints, the Virgin Mary, and Joseph hung on the wall. Doesticks wrote of the tackiness of these portraits, stating that Joseph was blue and being sold by "yellow brethren to a crowd of scarlet merchants who were paying for him with money that looked like peppermint lozenges."[3] He could hear Madame Widger before he could see her and was put off by her "shrill" laughter, which vibrated through the walls as she told another gentleman his fortune.

The man who greeted him at the door sank down in a chair and to Doesticks's offence tried to engage him in conversation. Apparently, the man had been involved in a number of dangerous voyages in his lifetime, including a trip involving the transporting of cheese and butter from Albany to New York City. Madame Widger's laughter ceased, and her client—who Doesticks surmised was a mason, based upon his cloudy boots and traces of lime on his pants—exited the room. On his first sight of the clairvoyant, Doesticks summed her up as a bony, tall, *very old* woman, with gray eyes and false teeth.

Madame Widger bade Doesticks to enter the "closet" where she was performing her trade. Once Doesticks was seated, Madame Widger informed him she charged a dollar for gentlemen and waited for Doesticks to produce the money before she would proceed. The transaction swiftly settled, she asked Doesticks to give her his left hand. She dabbed his palm four times and then opened a drawer in a nearby stand. A practitioner of lithomancy (a type of fortune telling using stones), Madame Widger took out a blue stone, examined it for a moment, then with her "vicious voice" told her customer that he was born under two planets, one of which was Mars, and that he would die under the planet Jupiter. Therefore, he would not die that particular year or the next, for that matter. His days of great trouble and misfortune were behind him, and the adventures he had had so far were enough to write an interesting book. She had intuited a storyteller in Doesticks.

Madame Widger then told him he would receive two letters, one a business letter, the other a letter from a friend. He would interact with a man who had light hair and blue eyes and would show great interest in him, but he should ultimately be wary of him. Doesticks would live to be sixty-eight, possibly seventy. When he was between thirty-two and thirty-four years old, he would lose a friend who would leave him a fortune.

Madame Widger then pulled another pebble out from her drawer and proclaimed after examining it that he would have two wives (a correct prediction), one blue-eyed, the other black-eyed. She then asserted he would have six children (an incorrect prediction). A man with light hair and blue eyes would try to get the first wife away from him, but he would not succeed. His first wife would be "good gentle kind loving affectionate true-hearted and pleasant."[4] Doesticks would be successful in business and be rich and happy.

She then took a Bible with a key tied to it. Madame Widger asked

Doesticks to take hold of the key with his finger, and he could make one wish. If the Bible turned, he would have his wish. As Doesticks took hold of the key, Madame Widger muttered something of which Doesticks could make no sense, "either a prayer or a recipe for pickling red cabbage,"[5] and the book turned, graciously granting Doesticks's wish.

At the close of the reading, Madame Widger presented him with a handbill that proclaimed: "Madame Widger was born with this wonderful gift of revealing the destinies of man, and she has revealed mysteries that no mortal knew. She states that she advertises nothing but what she can do with entire satisfaction to all who wish to consult her." Doesticks left the meeting unimpressed by this woman in her mid-forties who was old enough "to have been grandmother to his father's uncle."[6] Had either of Doesticks's wives lived to that age, would he have described them in similar terms?

His "good gentle kind loving affectionate true hearted and pleasant" wife now in the grave, and too preoccupied with his broken heart, Thomson may not have been reading the reviews and notices for *The Witches of New York* when it was released in December 1858 by Rudd & Carleton in New York and T. B. Peterson and Brothers in Philadelphia. His publisher had clearly spent money on advertising, anticipating brisk sales. Advertisements appeared in the press starting on its release date, across the United States, from Hartford, Connecticut, to Sonoma, California, and in such newspapers as the *New-York Tribune, Hartford Courant, Times Picayune, St. Johnsbury Caledonian, Louisville Daily Courier*, and *Sonoma County Journal*. Other newspapers as far afield as the *Pacific Commercial Advertiser* in Honolulu, Hawaii, noted receipt of the book. The cost of the book was one dollar, the same price as a one-on-one reading for a gentleman with Madame Widger.

Most reviews were complimentary, although there were fewer overall than there were for his first literary outing. The *New England Farmer* congratulated Doesticks on his work: "If the volume will be the means of stopping any of the cheats and frauds now practiced upon simple-hearted people, the author will deserve the thanks of the public."[7] On the same day, the *New York Times* also offered its stamp of approval, even going as far to suggest a good old-fashioned hanging for the loathsome fortune tellers.

The *Baton Rouge Tri-Weekly Gazette and Comet* also applauded Thomson's exposé: "It should admonish and deter. Fortune telling, in all its phases and varieties, is a gross imposture, and while its practice may be harmless in some instances, in others it is full of mischief, especially as it is calculated to disturb, the peace of families, to excite false expectations, to prompt and stimulate crime."[8] The *Times-Picayune* was complimentary: "Doesticks exposes, with his usual humor, but with straightforward honesty, the dangerous character and disgraceful, absurd business of the New York fortune-tellers, naming them and their localities, and freely exposing the whole system."[9]

As these notices began appearing, Thomson was freshly widowed, taking solace with his friends. Among them, he began spending more time with Van Cleve's close New York friend Grace Eldredge.

Eldredge was the daughter of Sara Payson Willis (who wrote under the pseudonym Fanny Fern) and Charles Harrington Eldredge, a Boston banker. Willis was born in Portland, Maine, in 1811, and was the daughter of the Reverend Nathaniel Willis, a newspaper owner and founder of the *Youth's Companion*, a weekly instructive periodical for children. She was also the sister of Nathaniel Parker Willis, who became a notable newspaper editor and journalist, famously editing works by Edgar Allan Poe and Henry Wadsworth Longfellow. Her younger brother, Richard Storrs Willis, wrote the melody of the Christmas carol "It Came upon the Midnight Clear." A spirited child, Sara attended a boarding school in Hartford, Connecticut, cofounded by Catharine Beecher (sister of Henry Ward Beecher and Harriet Beecher Stowe). Catherine Beecher would later tell Sara, "You were the worst behaved girl in my school . . . and I loved you the best."[10] Another letter from Harriet Beecher Stowe also revealed Willis's wild side at school, similar to Thomson's personality:

> I believe you have claim on a certain naughty girl once called Sarah Willis in whom I still retain an interest, who, I grieve to say one night stole a pie at Dr. Strongs and did feloniously excite unto sedition and rebellion some five or six other girls—eating said pie between eleven and twelve o'clock in defiance of the laws of the school and in breach of the peace—ask her if it isn't so—and if she remembers curling her hair with leaves from her geometry—perhaps she has long been penitent—[11]

At the age of twenty-six, Sara Willis married Charles Harrington Eldredge and later gave birth to three daughters: Mary Stace, Grace Harrington, and Ellen Willis. The eldest daughter, Mary, died of brain fever, which is now understood to be meningitis, and in the same year, 1845, Charles succumbed to typhoid fever. Now destitute, Sara received no help from her family, including her successful brother Nathaniel. Her father urged her to remarry, and in 1849 she reluctantly married the merchant Samuel P. Farrington. His behavior toward Willis was jealous and mentally abusive, and she scandalized society by leaving Farrington in 1851 and filing for divorce. She struggled to raise her two daughters on her paltry finances and was devastated to have to leave Grace to be brought up by her Eldredge grandparents.

In 1851, Willis published her first article in Boston's *Olive Branch* and followed up with more publications in the city's *True Flag*, all under the pseudonym of "Fanny Fern." The next year, she began writing in earnest, even sending articles to her brother Nathaniel, who told her she wouldn't be read outside Boston. As Julia Roberts would say in the 1990 film *Pretty Woman*, "Big mistake. Big. *Huge*."

Already growing in popularity by the summer of 1852, Fanny Fern was hired by the publisher Oliver Dyer at twice her salary to publish a regular column exclusively in the New York newspaper *Musical World and Times*. After working for the newspaper for over a year, her first two books were published: *Fern Leaves from Fanny's Portfolio* and *Little Ferns for Fanny's Little Friends*, a selection of her more sentimental columns as a children's book, both in 1853. *Fern Leaves* sold seventy thousand copies in its first year. Fanny Fern had become a phenomenon of her time.

Fern's work was then selected for publication in *Home Journal* by the untried author James Parton. *Home Journal* was owned by Fern's brother, Nathaniel, that same brother who said Fern would never be read outside Boston. Parton invited the mysterious Fanny Fern, whose identity had been subject to much gossip and speculation, to New York City. When her identity was revealed, Nathaniel told Parton he could no longer publish her work. Parton resigned in protest.

Robert Bonner, the publisher of the *New York Ledger*, had the novel idea of giving writers a byline in his newspaper so they could grow a following. Moreover, he could see that people were obsessed with the work of Fern. His initial offers to her to pen a weekly column were refused because she felt she was too busy. Finally, he offered one hundred dollars per column (about $3,600 in 2023), and Fern acquiesced. This made her the highest-paid columnist in the United States. At this point, Fern was making so much money in royalties from her first book and from her regular column that she bought herself a house in Brooklyn in 1855, where she could raise Ellen and Grace. Her novel *Ruth Hall*, a thinly disguised autobiography, recounted her happy years with Charles Eldredge, her destitution following his death, the lack of sympathy and help from family, and her eventual rise to fame. Her portrayal of her brother was highly unflattering.

Many male writers of the time dismissed her as "sentimental," but misogyny seems to have been well at work here; in fact, her writing is bold, snarky, outrageously hilarious, and passionate. She wrote unapologetically and energetically about such taboo topics of her time as equal pay, divorce, birth control, prostitution, venereal disease, the horrors of the insane asylum, cross-dressing, allowing a child to express their individuality, and more. She was the originator of the idiom "The way to a man's heart is through his stomach," though her original phrasing was "The straightest road to a man's heart is through his palate." The cover of her book *Fern Leaves* inspired the cover of Whitman's *Leaves of Grass*, and Fern was one of the first critics to praise the poet in a review of the initially controversial and misunderstood book. Fern was meticulous about meeting deadlines, and her final column appeared two days after she died. The last words in that column were, "Oh, God, I thank thee that I live."

By the mid-1850s, she had money and revenge and had attracted the admiration and love of Parton, an English-born writer, who had just published his first book, a biography of the newspaper editor and publisher Horace Greeley, and was working on a biography of Aaron Burr. While Fern felt affection toward Parton, she initially turned down his proposals of marriage, stating that she wished to maintain autonomy over her income and that she didn't believe marriage to be advantageous to women. Once Parton persuaded her that he had no intention of interfering with her career, success, or finances, and a prenuptial was signed, they married in 1856, and he moved into Fern's Brooklyn home, where she was living with her two daughters, Ellen and Grace. Louisa Matilda Jacobs, the daughter of Harriet Jacobs and author of *Incidents in the Life of a Slave Girl*, also lived with the family from July 1856 to April 1858.

According to the accounts of Thomas Butler Gunn, Grace was a bookish teenager. In 1857, he wrote that Grace was "a tall, fair haired girl of 16 or so, with an innocentish face, very fond of reading."[12] Gunn would also write of reading Charles Lamb and Lord Alfred Tennyson to her. Grace clearly shared her mother's rigorous intellect, talent for writing (she would publish articles in the *New-York Herald*), and penchant for dressing up in male clothing.

In June of the same year, Gunn ran into Willis and Parton and reported, "Fanny spake of a recent escapade of hers. How she put on a suit of Jim's clothes, and accompanied him in an evening's ramble through New York, dropping into a lager bier cellar, billiard room, &c and got weighed in a street-machine! Grace, too, had ventured on a mild promenade a la Amazon, in Brooklyn. Very American."[13] One might imagine the beer cellar to be Pfaff's, as it was known for tolerating such transgressive behavior.

Grace seems to have inherited her mother's feminist sensibilities. Under the pseudonym of Mrs. George Washington Wyllys, she wrote an article that sarcastically began, "It's so easy for a woman to be good natured! What cares has she beyond the hearth of home?"[14] In angry response to this sentiment, which had been expressed in an article she had recently read, Grace published the following diatribe:

> That paragraph was written by a man, depend on it! No woman ever penned such a piece of outrageous unreasonableness. . . . We know just how he looks—snuff-dried-solemn and sententious, and if ever we meet him on Broadway we shall identify straightaway, and take him to task for the above expression of his cankered sentiments! . . .
>
> We would cheerfully give up our very prettiest new bonnet for the privilege of taking a sly peep at you under the circumstances. Shouldn't we like to hear and see you grumbling because the tea-kettle has boiled over and burned your fingers?—shouldn't we enjoy seeing you dodge helplessly between the cradle and frizzling mutton chop on the fire, and wouldn't it be the height of human bliss, pre-mising that 'Biddy' had gone round the corner after a sixpennyworth of mustard, to behold your look of consternation on hearing the door bell announce a carriage-load of fashionable visitors just as you had plunged over-wrist-band-deep into the brine barrel in search of a small parallelogram of pork which contrives to elude your touch as deftly as if it were alive and instinct with mischief![15]

Given these feminist expressions, one wonders what Grace would have made of Doesticks's *Witches of New York*.

But as well as being fiery, Grace could be sweet, affectionate, and play-ful. Following a tiresome and grief-stricken day of mourning the death of Thomson's first wife on Christmas Eve, 1858, Gunn described the evening that followed: "A smoke and sleep and sunset, in Parton's room; talking with Fanny and the girls at evening, subsequently by 9 or later out to act as convoy to Grace who was bound to Dyer's for the purpose of leaving Christmas presents for the childrens Santa Claus-izing. A cold night, innu-merable stars out. You look just like Santa-Claus! said Grace."[16]

It was likely all these virtues that attracted the affections of Thomson.

Gunn was soon scandalized to learn that Thomson was courting Grace only three months after the death of his first wife. He had suspected something was brewing because he had seen Thomson sitting with Grace during his visits to the Fern household on Oxford Street, but he was also shocked that these developments were unfolding so openly and rapidly after Anna's death. Much later, he would reflect that it seemed the wooing had begun within a couple of weeks of the death of Chips, even though he mused in his diary that Thomson appeared to feel the death of his wife keenly. Perhaps he was eager to fill the void of loneliness. Gunn soon left the matter alone, using his diary to vent about Fanny Fern and how she had "manipulated" James Parton into marriage, though his dislike of Fern seemed to stem from the autonomy she held in the relationship.

In May of that year, Gunn would further rail that Grace would be a very different kind of wife than the one buried in Green-Wood. He wrote that Chips had adored Thomson without criticism, which was an admirable quality in a wife. Grace, however, was the daughter of the famous Fanny Fern, and that meant she would always consider her marriage to Thomson a step down. "He is not her ideal, I know," Gunn posited, "nor will he be able to place [her] in the position she will consider her due. She only recognizes newspaper men as a sort of addenda to her mother's fame, half-impatiently regarding them as shoppy."[17] But the romance did not seem to be as doomed as Gunn originally thought. On June 20, 1859, he commented, "Mort's wooing goes on, he writing and receiving a prodigiously long love-letter every day of his life. All his evenings are spent with Grace."[18]

It seems the marriage was more than one of mutual intellect and affection; for Thomson it was also a marriage of means. Not only did he need money, but Gunn also hinted that Thomson's mother, Sophia, was tickled by the match because her son would come into fame and fortune as the son-in-law of Fanny Fern. "Mort is shrewd and politic," Gunn observed. "Grace has or will have money, too, in addition to the incitements of passion which Mort may be fairly presumed to feel for her."[19]

Thomson's childhood friend Ed Wells came to visit later that June, and Gunn reported that he seemed to fuss over Thomson with the attention of a lover. "He is an extreme type," Gunn observed, and was apparently a lot more attentive to Thomson's needs than Grace. Gunn continued his calumny, "Knowing Mort Thomson from boyhood, his friendship for him verges on the morbid, manifesting itself in such ministrations as no man ought to offer to or accept from another, as tying his cravat, cutting up his meat, brushing his clothes &c, all of which His Grace of Doesticks accords, no doubt with real regard for his worshipper."[20] If this is an accurate portrayal, the two men did seem to harbor an unusually intimate and affectionate relationship.

In the meantime, Mark Thomson, Mortimer's first child, had been whisked away to Minnesota in November 1859 to be with his maternal grandmother. Grace did not seem interested in raising a child who was not her own, and Thomson appeared, at that point, to have had little interest in the boy since his birth.

Now unburdened by child, in November 1859 Thomson went on his "Pluck" lecture tour, visiting various Northeastern and Midwestern states. "Pluck" was a humorous lecture-poem, written on the advent of the Civil War, to inspire courage in fellow supporters of the Union. In 1883, his brother Clifford had private copies of the lecture printed to circulate among relatives, and in its introduction, he wrote, "He seldom read it twice alike, constantly changing and adding to it, making it conform to public events as they transpired. The incidents of the civil war were fruitful topics with him and in addition to this lecture, he has left abundant evidence of his unswerving patriotism and enthusiastic love for the Union cause."[21] The *New-York Tribune* praised the lecture, stating that "Mr. Thomson handles his subject with much humor, interspersed with many new and forcibly-put ideas."[22] Gunn, however, wrote that "Pluck" was "awful bosh, old puns, old stale satire, irrelevance and what not, with here and there a bit of strong truth, but nothing that hasn't been said a hundred times better."[23]

Gunn's next mention of the courting couple came on August 3, 1860, when he spotted Fern, Parton, Eldredge, and Thomson on board a boat bound for Rochester for a summer getaway. Gunn's suggestions of impropriety concerning the courtship seem overly unfair, however, as the couple did not wed until May 12, 1861, almost two and a half years after Anna's death. Fern had since moved to a townhouse on Eighteenth Street in Manhattan, where the marriage took place. It was a simple ceremony becoming of the times, as the country was on the brink of war. It was conducted by Henry Ward Beecher. At that point, Thomson had moved from Brooklyn to Manhattan and was living at 168 East Twenty-First Street, likely so his bride could live closer to her parents. Gunn wrote, "The ceremony was of the briefest, not occupying twenty minutes, Grace wearing the $100 dress of lilac silk. . . . She went through it well, looking like a honest school girl and appearing perfectly unaffected."[24] Witnesses who signed the certificate were Thomson's pals Ed Wells and J. C. Haney, the publisher of the *Comic Monthly*, who married Parton's cousin Martha Edwards.

Gunn did not harbor high hopes for the marriage, which he predicted would be an "average one."[25] He believed Thomson would take Grace to the theater, talk with exaggeration, get drunk, and work hard. Thomson had a coarse nature, and Gunn was convinced that Grace would never truly come to love him. Gunn was not alone in his queasy feelings about the marriage. On March 30, 1861, shortly after Thomson had requested Grace's hand in marriage and she had given permission, Fern published an article in the *Ledger* that began:

> How any young fellow can have the face to walk into your family, and deliberately ask for one of your daughters, passes me. That it is done every day, does not lessen my astonishment at the sublime impudence of the thing. There you have been, sixteen, or seventeen, or eighteen years of her life, combing her hair, and washing her face for—*him!*[26]

Considering the events that transpired in the year following the marriage, it would seem Fanny Fern was not at all wrong to have misgivings.

While Thomson's second love match was not a resounding success, Madame Widger appeared to have been making unsuccessful matches herself. In addition to being engaged in the trade of fortune telling, she offered her services as a marriage broker. On April 22, 1871, Thomson's paper, the *New-York Tribune*, ran an exposé headlined "The Vilest of Women." The article explored the services of Madame Ross, Madame Clara, Madame Jones, and Madame Widger. According to the report, Madame Widger was running a "matrimonial office" near Fourteenth Street, where the reporter made his way up "two flights of rickety stairs." Upon meeting Madame Widger, the reporter described her face as having "the meanest kind of cunning combined with a lewd indifference or defiance of everything pure or decent." Not only was her face displeasing, but her voice also had "a sharp nasal twang, her eyes are restless and malignant, and her whole manner is such that had she lived 200 years ago, the stake would have been in instant requisition."[27] Like Doesticks, this reporter likened Madame Widger to a witch, advocating for the return of medieval torture of her kind.

Initially the author had told Madame Widger that he was there to have his fortune told and that she had rattled off "a long list of absurdly improbable events, each sentence beginning with 'I see.'"[28] The reporter then inquired after Madame Widger's matrimonial business, asking about the young ladies who were to be matched by her. Madame Widger replied that she managed them and that although it was a little difficult and required several visits, in the end they would come around. Madame Widger told him that ultimately a photograph of the gentleman was the best persuasion for the young lady to agree to a meeting. The reporter then asked if the young ladies would prefer not to leave their homes in that way, presumably without the knowledge or permission of the family, to which Madame Widger replied that some of them didn't, but others came from homes in which they felt they were not treated right by their parents and looked forward to the opportunity to leave. The reporter was working under the assumption that the young ladies who approached Madame Widger were from "respectable" and happy homes.

Madame Widger then excused herself by saying her daughter was attending a ball that night, and she wanted to check on her appearance. A moment later she returned with a young lady "from 17 to 18 years of age."[29] The young lady stood looking at the reporter and then nodded to her mother and went out. The reporter was apparently naïvely perplexed by this maneuver. The session ended with Madame Widger promising the reporter to see what she could do to find him a young lady, and she would write to him to come back some day at the beginning of the following week.

Madame Widger's matrimonial services were legendary among newspapers. This account was reprinted in such newspapers as the *Times Picayune*. The *Norfolk Virginian* published its own discussion of Madame Widger's matrimonial services on May 5, 1871. In this article, Madame Widger had informed the reporter that she had the names of twenty young ladies registered. "You needn't let the name 'matrimonial' frighten you," she said, "of course it has to come under that head, and once in a while two persons will marry." The reporter expressed concern about the supervision of the arrangements, to which Madame Widger replied, "When the gentleman comes again, I tell him to go around and see her; and if he likes her, why after a while they generally go off together. I don't know where they go to; it isn't any of my business." At the conclusion of the report, the writer condemned the women making these matrimonial arrangements in no uncertain terms, calling them "the lowest estimate of human character."[30]

What might have been behind some of these newspapers' attacks of and investigations into these matchmakers? In her 2020 book *Matrimony, Inc.*, Francesca Beauman documents the advent of the first personal ad in the United States and later their burgeoning popularity. "Marriage ads reached their apogee in mid-19th century New York," she writes.[31] Among the newspapers profiting from this phenomenon were the *New York Herald* and the *New York Times*. The rise of personal ads was essentially a result of the competitive rivalry between New York's penny presses, including the *New York Sun*, *New York Herald*, and *New-York Tribune*, all of which were looking for titillating ways to attract their readers. Ads were so important to the newspapers of the day that often the first two pages of the eight-page *New-York Tribune* were nothing but ads. The expansion of respectable wage work for New York women into fields such as retail and teaching allowed women a certain amount of economic independence from their parents and more notably allowed them to flout social conventions, such as the "correct way" to find a husband. Madame Widger, in the article, had also noted this phenomenon. Women wanted to date without having the restrictive supervision of their parents, who were often overbearing.

In 1861, one New York editor sang the praises of the personal ads: "Who is there who does not read the 'Personals' of the *Herald*, and who can read them without having his mind directed into channels of romance? [T]his column of the daily newspaper contains within itself a most curious phantasmagoria of city life, and those who have a taste for real romance need go no farther to gratify it."[32] The *Tribune* writer conducting his interview of Madame Widger was apparently scandalized that she was not chaperoning her clients on their dates, but were the newspapers following through to see that relationships formed out of personal ads were decently conducted and concluded in harmonious matrimony? It is possible that the *Tribune* may have been more interested in besmirching Madame Widger's character because she was a competitor.

Curiously, one of the strongest critics of the personal ad was Fanny Fern. In the *New York Herald*, she condemned the behavior of women seeking out a marriage match in the personals: "There is no necessity for an attractive, or, to use a hateful phrase, a 'marketable' woman, to take such a degrading step. . . . A woman must first have ignored the sweetest attributes of womanhood, have overstepped the last barrier of self-respect, who would parley with a stranger on such a topic."[33]

In the same year as the *New-York Tribune* exposé on her, 1871, Madame Widger appeared in the press again. This time, her story was not the focus of the article but instead used her association with a young lady to discredit the reputation of the subject. The headline of the article in the *Beatrice Weekly Express* was "A Fifteen-Year-Old Husband." The story started by introducing a situation that had been presented in court. A Mrs. Kate Palmer was suing her husband, John Palmer, in the Essex Market Police Court for abandonment. John Palmer was only seventeen years old, according to his mother, and he had been married for two years. He had a one-year-old child with Kate Palmer. The couple had met "some years ago,"[34] when Kate Palmer (then Kate Laundsbury) was working as a chambermaid at 783 Greenwich Street, the Palmer home. No mention is made in the article of Kate's age.

The family later moved to 156 West Eleventh Street, taking Kate with them. The servants noticed John Palmer's attentions toward Kate, but the parents were apparently oblivious. Eventually, the cook mentioned to her mistress that Kate was trying to "inveigle her son." In response, the mother sought to remove her son from the household by sending him out west to live with her uncle, but the boy returned three weeks later. There was a theory that Kate sent him money (which seems unlikely, given the paltry salary Kate was probably earning). Kate remained in her position, and shortly after John returned from his trip, he and Kate married privately at a Catholic church on Second Street by the Reverend Father Everett. The parents, who claimed to be surprised and shocked by the union, sent Kate away, providing her with lodgings and maintenance.

The family moved to Port Richmond, Rhode Island, where the mother kept the Continental Hotel, while the father commuted to the city to continue conducting his business. John would send twelve to fifteen dollars weekly to Kate but eventually stopped, leaving Kate in the precarious position of having to find work to support herself. She went to work for Mrs. Dancliffson, at whose home she would also live.

The lawyers for John Palmer had attempted to smear Kate's character, as apparently the first person she had recognized in court was "the notorious Mme. Widger, the clairvoyant."[35] It is not clear from the article what Madame Widger was doing in court or how Kate came to recognize her. She had met John as the son of her employer, not through Madame Widger's matrimonial services.

The judge ultimately dismissed these attempts to discredit Kate and decreed that if Kate remained John's wife, he must pay four dollars a week for support. The mother declared her intention to immediately file for the divorce of Kate and John. Whatever happened next in this story did not appear in any newspaper.

One of the striking things about this episode is the mother's refusal to acknowledge her son's responsibility in the courtship of Kate or his responsibility as a husband and the father of the child. Nor did the mother consider herself culpable for her part in allowing the situation to evolve to the point it had. Why was she "surprised" by the secret marriage following her son's return from the West after three weeks? Why did she not remove him to Rhode Island then? Or fire Kate from her position? Or even better, work toward finding Kate a new situation or sharing responsibility in the raising of her grandchild? This story further demonstrates the frustrating situation in which working women found themselves: Men were not held culpable for their actions, while women in vulnerable positions bore the brunt of responsibility, as well as any moral ire following public scandal.

Perhaps Madame Widger's reputation was so renowned at the trial because of all the fortune tellers, she appears to be the most consistent and regular in her profession. Advertisements for her fortune telling and matrimonial services appeared in newspapers starting in 1855 and continued until 1878, around the same time that she disappeared from the *New York City Directory*. Either she retired, found a new profession, or changed her identity, but most likely she died. She would have been sixty-five in 1878, a likely age of death for an impoverished woman of that era.

Madame Widger also maintained the most consistent addresses. From 1861 to 1870, she advertised her address at 165 Bowery. Her last listed address was 179 Eighth Avenue, a short walk from where Grace Eldredge took her last breath.

Chapter 5

▟▛

Mr. Grommer

Lenormand Card: Ship (Meaning = *Travel*)

When this article was originally published in the *New-York Tribune* on May 9, 1857, it was titled "Mrs. Grommer," even though Doesticks ultimately received his reading from a *Mr.* Grommer.[1] He would later title the fourteenth chapter of his book "Mr. Grommer," but this is a good example of how Doesticks rigorously continued to characterize fortune telling as a female domain, even though men would occasionally dabble in fortune telling as both readers and clients.

Neither Mr. nor Mrs. Grommer advertised their fortune telling services in the newspapers. Doesticks heard through his gossip grapevine that a *Mrs.* Grommer in Williamsburgh was a gifted seer, and that led him to peg Mrs. Grommer as the kind of fortune teller who offers her services not as a full-time profession but out of friendship. Nonetheless, Doesticks speculated, even if Mrs. Grommer did consent to the occasional reading for a friend, she would no doubt charge the going rate. "Many of them combine fortune-telling with hard work," Doesticks observed, "and do their full day's work of faithful toil at some legitimate employment, and in the evening amuse themselves with witchcraft."[2] According to Doesticks, Mrs. Grommer was putting aside her day job more and more to practice her magical knowledge, though where Doesticks obtained this information is never revealed.

This chapter depicted the first time Doesticks ventured to Williamsburgh, formerly its own municipality. Although the *h* at the end of its name was dropped in 1855 when it became part of Brooklyn, Doesticks continued to spell it the earlier way. With no advertisement to direct him, simply word of mouth, he made his way unannounced to No. 34 North Second Street. Doesticks does not say how he got there, but it is possible that he walked north from his Brooklyn address on Hoyt Street, a brisk one-hour walk, or he may have taken a stagecoach line.

Those who recommended Mrs. Grommer to Doesticks described her as living in a "cave." With characteristic hyperbole, Doesticks fantasized what this cave might be like. Drawing comparisons with the Witch of Vesuvius, he imagined a woman with lank, gray, dead hair, stony eyes, and blue lips. He envisioned her accompanied by a red-eyed fox, a crested serpent, and surrounded by the skulls of a dog, a horse, and a boar. Excited by these imaginings, Doesticks arrived at the "enchanted" spot only to find another impoverished and industrialized area. The "cave" turned out to be a drinking saloon with a billiard room. Instead of finding snakes and foxes, Doesticks encountered working-class men drinking beer and spirits. He asked after Mrs. Grommer at the saloon and was sent up an irregular and crooked street that took him half an hour to ascend by foot. Doesticks described the environs as follows:

> The grading of the street has left at this point a gravel bank some six or eight feet high, on the summit of which is perched the house of Mrs. Grommer, like a contented mud-turtle on a sunny stump. It is a one-story affair, with several irregular wings or additions sprouting out of it at unexpected angles, and, on the whole, it looks as if it had been originally built tall and slim like a tallow candle, but had been melted and run down into its present indescribable shape. The architect neglected to provide this beautiful edifice with a front door, and the inquirer was compelled to ascend the bank by a flight of rheumatic steps, and make a grand detour through currant bushes, chickens, washtubs, rain-barrels, and colored children, irregular as to size, and variegated as to hue, to the back, and only door.[3]

Upon arrival at the Grommer household, Doesticks noted Mrs. Grommer, a Black woman, scolding what he assumed to be her grandchildren for trespassing on the currant bushes of a neighbor. Imagine—the hipster Williamsburg neighborhood we know today was hilly farmland and industry in 1857. Mrs. Grommer gave those children a spanking, which drew the cheers of neighbors.

While Mrs. Grommer disciplined her grandchildren, Doesticks observed the house in which they lived. There was a reception room of about ten feet by twelve, with a roof so low it would present a challenge to a tall man. The room was "dingily carpeted" and contained a double bed, a cooking stove, seven chairs of varied patterns, a pack of cards upon a small round table, and a chest of drawers, as well as a black wooden cross and miniature casts of lambs and dogs. This was not the wild-eyed witchy scene Doesticks had hoped for. Rather it was a cozy and humble abode.

Doesticks made himself comfortable, and when Mrs. Grommer entered the room, he sized her up, estimating her to be about sixty-five and weighing around two hundred pounds. Doesticks told Mrs. Grommer his purpose, but to his surprise, she adamantly insisted she did not read for gentlemen. Doesticks entreated her, and she refused to budge. A Black woman refusing a white man service in the antebellum era—this is remarkable. Fortune telling allowed even women of color to have some level of autonomy over their profession and the money they earned.

Eventually, Mrs. Grommer advised Doesticks that her husband would do it but emphasized he would charge a dollar, no less. Doesticks agreed to Mrs. Grommer's terms and waited while she fetched Mr. Grommer to tell Doesticks his future. When Mr. Grommer arrived, Doesticks described him as "a shrewd-looking old man, with a dash of white blood in his composition; his hair curls tightly all over his head, but is elaborated on each side of his face into a single hard-twisted ringlet; short crisped whiskers, streaked with grey, encircle his face, and an imperial completes his hirsute attractions; his cheeks and forehead are marked with the small-pox."[4]

Mr. Grommer commenced shuffling the cards and sized Doesticks up correctly, telling him he could see he didn't believe in the cards. Nonetheless he persisted, perceiving that Doesticks had lost something bright and round that hung on a nail. He told Doesticks that he lived in a boarding house with two girls and that he had wrongly accused one of them of taking the object. But he had blamed the wrong girl; the light-haired girl had taken it. When Doesticks arrived home that day, he should look under the mattress, as perhaps the guilty party had put it back. If not, Doesticks should confront her, because it was in the house. Of course, none of this made any sense to Doesticks.

Mr. Grommer continued stabbing in the dark with his predictions. Doesticks would be going on a journey soon. He would receive a lot of money from overseas but would also have a disappointment. He was born under a lucky star. He would be married soon but would have disappointment from his first wife. The father didn't like Doesticks because he was too "dark complected." Doesticks should not marry the first lady. He should marry the second lady, who looked like the Queen of Diamonds. This statement implies Mr. Grommer may have been telling fortunes with a pack of plain playing cards, which is not that unusual, considering that fortune telling cards evolved from playing cards.

The original article ends with Mrs. Grommer entering the room to observe the conclusion of the reading. Mr. Grommer told his client that he had seen a great deal of trouble and that there was more to come, but that his last days would be his best days. He would live a long life, though Mr. Grommer could not predict exactly how long. Doesticks was again unimpressed by the reading. In his book, he concluded the Grommer chapter simply with: "He condescended no more, and the Cash Customer disbursed his dollar and departed, all the grandchildren gathering on the bank to give him three cheers as a parting salute."[5]

Thomson's sympathies were undoubtedly with the abolition movement. During the Civil War, he would fight with the Union. The biggest indicator of his values, however, is the article-turned-booklet that followed *The Witches of New York*. It was written several months after the death of Anna Van Cleve, perhaps as a way of channeling his grief. The story first appeared in article form in the *New-York Tribune* on March 9, 1859, and it covered the sale of Pierce Butler's slaves in Savannah, Georgia, telling the raw story in all its horror. The article was dripping in sarcasm and sub-headlined, "Human feelings of no account—Mr. Butler gives each chattel a dollar."[6]

The sale, identified to be the largest one to have taken place in the United States, was located at Ten Broek Race Course, in Savannah, Georgia, a rapidly growing city. Between 1840 and 1860, Savannah's population had doubled, from 11,214 to 22,292. With the construction of the Central Railroad of Georgia, originally running 190 miles between Savannah and Macon (likely a route ridden by Madame Clifton) and later expanding to Tennessee and Alabama, it was drawing more people from all over the country. By 1860, it had surpassed Charleston in cotton exports. Its narrow streets, lanes, and alleys, poor gas lighting, and exotic mix of Spanish daggers, magnolias, palmettos, and Spanish moss hanging ghostly from trees made it an eerie and haunting place. Just a few months before the slave auction, the ship *Wanderer* had arrived off the coast of Georgia from the Congo, disguised as a luxury cruise liner, with four hundred slaves smuggled on board. During the trip, eighty slaves had perished, and at the time of the auction, the crewmembers of the *Wanderer* were awaiting trial for violating the federal Slave Importation Act. A common sight in Savannah, one likely witnessed by Thomson, was coffles of handcuffed Black men, women, and children, who were transported twice a week from pens owned by traders.

The lot of slaves to be sold at Ten Broek consisted of 436 men, women, and children. Pierce Mease Butler and his brother John had inherited their grandfather Major Pierce Butler's plantations, and the properties had been split between them. Pierce favored spending his fortune on cards, and with his gambling debts growing as rapidly as the population of Savannah, a group of trustees was formed in 1856 to seize his assets. The trustees had placed bad investments in the stock market, and soon thereafter the Panic of 1857 had compounded those losses. In order to raise money to cover Butler's debts and the dwindling stock, the trustees decided they would sell his half of the slaves on the property.

The sale was managed by Joseph Bryan, a "Negro Broker," who was apparently thronged by anxious inquirers daily. Thomson identified the buyers as a "rough breed, slangy, profane and bearish, being for the most part from the back river and swamp plantations, where the elegancies of polite life are not perhaps developed to their fullest extent." In fact, Thomson would say that their best knowledge of luxuries merely extended to revolvers and other "kindred delicacies." Posing as an interested buyer, Thomson concealed his identity at the sale because, as he put it euphemistically, he did not want to be "the recipient of a public demonstration from the enthusiastic Southern population, who at times overdo their hospitality and their guests."[7]

There were no light mulattoes, Thomson observed, but then he took on the voice of a Southern plantation owner and noted with sarcasm, "The pure-blooded negroes are much more docile and manageable than mulattoes, though less quick of comprehension, which makes them preferred by drivers, who can stimulate stupidity by the lash much easier than they can control intelligence by it." It was noted that none of the slaves had been sold before, and therefore there were families among the slaves who had never been apart. "And who can tell how closely intertwined are the affections of a little band of four hundred persons living isolated from all the world beside, from birth to middle age?" Thomson pondered. "Do they not naturally become one great family, each man a brother unto each?" Thomson further noted that while it was claimed some were sold in family units, those family units might just be defined as husband and wife and not include brothers and sisters, parents and kindred. "And the separation is as utter, and is infinitely more hopeless, than that made by the angel of death."[8]

The slaves were transported to the racecourse and sequestered in sheds normally reserved for horses and carriages. They carried no more possessions than scanty articles of clothing and tin dishes and gourds for food and drink. Though none of the slaves wept, their faces betrayed a heavy grief. The children were of various ages and sizes; the youngest was just fifteen days old. While enslaved people mainly worked at planting rice and cotton, some were skilled in mechanics. There were also coopers,[9] carpenters, shoemakers, and blacksmiths.

Thomson wrote of the inhumane and undignified manner with which the buyers addressed the slaves. One slave, whose name was Molly, was spoken to in the following manner: "Show mas'r yer arm, Molly—good arm dat, mas'r—she do a heap of work mo' with dat arm yet. Let good mas'r see yer teeth Molly—see dat Mas'r, teeth all reg'lar, all good—she'm young gal yet."[10] He then turned his attention to Molly's child. This energized Molly to begin bargaining and pleading with the potential buyer to take them both. While it was stated at the opening of the auction that the enslaved would be sold in "families"—that is, a man would not be parted from his wife and a "young child" not parted from its mother—what was defined as a "young child" is not recorded. Molly was right to be concerned.

It rained violently over the course of the two days of the dismal sale, which later earned it the name "The Weeping Time," as though the heavens were sobbing at the inhumanity of it all. Those who were to be sold were mounted on a platform, and those who were not likely to be immediately wanted were gathered into "sad groups" in the background to watch the progress of the proceedings. About two hundred buyers clustered around, lighting their cigars and readying their catalogs and pencils.

While mingling among the buyers, Thomson picked up on the most disturbing conversation: ' "If a nigger really sets himself up against me, I can't never have any patience with him. I just get my pistol and shoot him right down." These were the auctioneers to whom the enslaved were to be sold. Thomson noted a mood of "crushed hopes and broken hearts." Women were lewdly commented upon. Suggestively, the buyers often questioned why certain women were "covered up." Thomson wrote that some of them made remarks "too indecent and obscene to be even hinted at here."[11] One can only imagine the fate of these women. The auctioneer commented that the lady and her child needed to be covered up by a shawl because of the wind and the rain.

In the last section of the article, Thomson homed in on individual cases that further uncovered the horrors of selling human beings. One such person on the auctioneering block was a young lady called Daphney, who had recently given birth on Valentine's Day. After traveling from the plantation to Savannah, she had been kept in a shed for six days. She had then been subjected to questioning and insults from speculators, and then on the fifteenth day, she was showcased on the block with her husband, other child, and newborn baby. Thomson sarcastically wrote, "It was very considerate in Daphney to be sick before the sale, for her wailing babe was worth to Mr. Butler all of a hundred dollars."[12]

Among the others who were sold were two newlyweds; a mother and her twin boys; a twenty-three-year-old man, Jeffrey, who was forced to be separated from his sweetheart, Dorcas, the woman to whom he was to have been betrothed; Violet, who was suffering from consumption (known today as tuberculosis); and a lame woman called Molly, who was subjected to much embarrassment to prove she was in fact unable to walk without great pain and difficulty.

In the final passage, adding insult to injury, Pierce Butler made his way among his sold-off slaves, giving them a dollar a piece for their hard work over the years. After two days of this cruelty, Doesticks noted that the clouds broke away and sunlight reappeared. He poetically concluded: "But the stars shone out as brightly as if such things had never been, the blushing fruit trees poured their fragrance on the evening air, and the scene was as calmly sweet and quiet as if Man had never marred the glorious beauties of Earth by deeds of cruelty and wrong."[13]

Thomson told the story of the Pierce Mease Butler slaves at great risk to his personal safety. Had he revealed himself to be a reporter from the North, not only would no one have talked to him, but, given the threats sent to newspapers, it is likely he would have suffered personal injury. Ethel Parton detailed in a letter to Daniel Fletcher Slater that her father had indeed undertaken this journalistic endeavor to his personal peril: "An actor acquaintance of that period once recognized him when he was reporting disguised as a Southern farmer in the South, and for old times sake warn him that he was suspected and helped him get away in time. This, I have always supposed, was the same occasion as the Pierce-Butler sale; but I do not know certainly that it was."[14] On March 16, 1859, Thomas Butler Gunn commented in his diary, "While at the house, Mort Thomson and Cahill came, the latter having that day returned from Savannah whither he went to report a great slave sale for the Tribune. Marry, the Georgians would have tarred, feathered and ridden him on a rail had they known his mission! Mort did the writing out a whole Tribune pig page of print, in the railroad cars smart reporting."[15]

On March 25, 1859, the *Richmond Dispatch* wrote, "The person who reported six columns of misrepresentations of a sale of 436 negroes at Savannah, Ga., for the New York Tribune, was Mortimer Thomson, ('Doesticks,') who is attached to that paper, and was sent to Savannah for the purpose. He left town the day after the sale, and wrote his report on the cars. It is a pity the Georgians didn't know the object of his errand and his name."[16] This report had a tone of mild threat in it. The *Athens Post*, in Georgia, was harsher. "It seems that 'Doesticks' is the author of the report of the sale of slaves in Charleston, which appeared recently in the New York Tribune. The New York News says: 'If 'Doesticks' suffers himself to get mixed in the 'nigger business,' many persons will be convinced that he and 'Damphool' are one and the same individual."[17]

Thomson's article would later be reissued in booklet form after the release of a related publication in 1863. Pierce Butler had married a British Shakespearean actress, Frances Anne Kemble, in 1834. It had been a tumultuous marriage; Kemble was a strong-willed woman, and Butler had hoped to tame her independent nature in marriage. Shortly following the birth of their two daughters, Butler inherited half of his grandfather's plantations. Kemble had repeatedly asked to see them, having only heard of the horrors of slavery at home in England. Butler had a rice plantation on a 1,500-acre island in the Altamaha River and a cotton plantation on the north end of Saint Simons Island. Butler finally agreed to have Kemble tour the plantations between 1838 and 1839, and she found the conditions on them even more horrifying and callous than she imagined. She kept a journal during her time there.

In 1849, Butler and Kemble divorced. A custody battle for their two daughters followed, and once the two daughters came "of age," Kemble published her journal in 1863 as *Journal of a Residence on a Georgia Plantation (1838–1839)*. It both scandalized and galvanized the Union Army, and interest in the story was strong enough to prompt the republication of Thomson's article in booklet form, with the title *What Became of the Slaves on a Georgia Plantation? Great Auction Sale of Slaves at Savannah, Georgia, March 2d & 3d, 1859, a Sequel to Mrs. Kemble's Journal.*

This once famous sale is now largely forgotten. In 2008, a plaque acknowledging the auction was dedicated in the vicinity of the race course, which has long since been torn down. The area is mainly populated by houses and churches; the plaque stands in a depressed tiny triangular park area near a bus stop.

Shortly following the publication of Mrs. Kemble's journal, New York City would see one of its most disgraceful chapters, which Thomson would also witness. The New York City Draft Riots took place from July 13 to 16, 1863. The rioters were mainly Irish immigrants (or those of Irish descent) aggrieved by the unfair policies of the recent Civil War draft, as well as fear that they were having to compete for labor with recently freed Blacks. The latest draft rules had decreed that anyone could buy their way out of the draft for three hundred dollars (approximately $6,100 in 2020). This outraged the impoverished Irish population, who could not afford such a luxury. Moreover, as they were ineligible for citizenship, Black people were also not being drafted, which added a further note of tension. What commenced as understandable anger over the inequities of the draft quickly degenerated into nightmarish violence against the city's Black population and any person or business supporting abolition. The rioting went on for several days.

On July 13, as the mob made its way further uptown, it was suggested that the rioters should attack the Colored Orphan Asylum on Fifth Avenue between Forty-Third and Forty-Fourth streets. There were 233 children seated in the schoolrooms at the time the mob descended on the building, taking bedding, clothing, and food before setting fire to it. Although the fire department was on hand, they were unable to save the building, and it burned down in twenty minutes. The superintendent and matron of the asylum had miraculously been able to assemble the children and escort them out the back entrance onto Forty-Fourth Street. The children were taken into protection at the Thirty-Fifth Police Precinct station, where they remained for three days before being moved to the almshouse on Blackwell's Island.

At one point during the attack on the asylum, an Irish observer called out, "If there is a man among you, with a heart within him come and help these poor children." The mob laid hold of him and appeared ready to tear him to pieces. Other white people who came under attacks of various kinds included Abby Hopper Gibbons, a prison reformer and daughter of an abolitionist; Ann Derrickson and Ann Martin, who were married to Black men; and Mary Burke, a white prostitute who catered to Black men.

At the time, Thomson was living at 80 East Seventeenth Street in Manhattan. He witnessed an elderly, colored woman fleeing from rioters, so he rushed to seize a revolver and ran out into the street, where he took the terrified woman by the arm and pointed his pistol at the mob. He kept the men at bay until he had led the woman to safety at the local stationhouse, three blocks from his house.[18]

Williamsburgh emerged in the 1850s as an exciting place of industrial development and rapid change. It shared its evolution with the nearby neighborhoods of Greenpoint, Wallabout Bay (by the Navy Yard), and Gowanus Bay. It hosted iron foundries, white-lead factories, steam-powered ropeworks, the first Pfizer plant, distilleries, and the Havemeyer sugar plant. On April 7, 1851, it declared itself the City of Williamsburgh. It grew to six times its population in just a decade, reaching thirty thousand in 1850. It attracted Irish and German immigrants, as well as freed slaves who sometimes lived in small shantytowns.

The Grommers have been the most difficult to trace of all the fortune tellers. As was mentioned in *The Witches of New York*, neither Mr. nor Mrs. Grommer advertised their services. The name Grommer was a rare one in the 1850s. In fact, a simple search for the name Grommer in New York State came up with only a handful of hits over a span of thirty years. On Ancestry.com, the name Grommer appears in census records a total of 210 times. The last name of Grommer appears on forty-eight passenger lists in immigration records, and there are only a total of fifty-nine military records using the name Grommer. The name was commonly associated with farmers and male laborers. In the city directories of that era, a Michael Grommer is noted to be a peddler living at 179 Third Avenue in 1869–1870. Another listing for "D. Grommer (col'd)" had the occupation of "washing" and an address at 265 Rivington Street.[19] There is no evidence to connect that Grommer with the fortune teller met by Doesticks. There are several reasons that the Grommer family of Williamsburgh is so difficult to find. They were working class, poor, and Black.

The 1850s were a unique time for Black people like the Grommers living in New York City. While slavery had been abolished in 1827 in New York State, it had not been eradicated nationwide. Moreover, much of the city's wealth and exponential growth had been on the backs of Black people. Cotton was a crop picked by southern slaves but financed by Wall Street banks. It was shipped to New England and British textile mills via the monetary power of New York brokers, businesses, and investors. Further, slave masters were reliant upon New York insurance companies to safeguard their assets in bondage, and they welcomed the credit extended by the city's banks. While New York had abolished slavery, it was still economically dependent upon it; this is why it so often turned a blind eye to the sinister actions of such organizations as the "Kidnapping Club." This was not an organized institution or even a social club. Rather, it was an attitude and tacit agreement among the city's prominent officials, including police officers, political authorities, judges, lawyers, and slave traders, who did not care about the particulars of the law regarding whether they arrested an escaped slave or someone born free. Businesspeople of New York often stood in moral support of attempts to return fugitive slaves to the South because they were still dependent on its slave economy. The scholar Leslie M. Harris wrote that antebellum writers estimated New Yorkers earned as much as forty cents on every dollar's worth of southern cotton sold.[20] Black activists such as David Ruggles often found themselves fighting against the New York press; for example, he once sued a man who was illegally holding an enslaved Black person in New York. Papers such as the *New York Express* stated that Ruggles would "embarrass trade," and the *New York Gazette* similarly wrote disparagingly of Ruggles, who, it claimed, flouted fugitive slave laws and disobeyed racial boundaries.

The scholar Jonathan Daniel Wells wrote in his book *The Kidnapping Club* that two police officers, Tobias Boudinot and Daniel D. Nash, were key players in terrorizing Black New Yorkers by sending them to the South with slave owners, regardless of whether they were former slaves or free. These circumstances are also documented in Solomon Northup's *Twelve Years a Slave*. There is a possibility that the Grommers were keeping a low profile perhaps because they were escaped slaves or feared being kidnapped.

The year 1857, when Thomson visited the Grommers, was a significant one for Black people. It was the year of the Dred Scott decision. In March of that year, the US Supreme Court held that the US Constitution was not meant to include American citizenship for people of African descent, whether enslaved or free. The decision was made in the case of Dred Scott, who was enslaved in Missouri. His owners had taken him from Missouri to Illinois and the Wisconsin Territory, where slavery was illegal. Scott tried to sue his owners for his freedom when they brought him back to Missouri because he had been taken into free territory, which should have made him automatically free. His first suit in Missouri had been unsuccessful, so Scott had sued in US federal court, which ultimately ruled against him. The decision had ripple effects in the Black community, as it essentially established that those who had escaped from slavery were not safe anywhere.

As one example of this, Lewis Howard Latimer, an African American inventor and electrical pioneer, was born in 1848 to parents who had formerly been enslaved in Virginia. His father, George, ran away to freedom to Boston in October 1842, with his wife, Rebecca, who had been the slave of another man. When the owner, James B. Gray, appeared in Boston to take them back to Virginia, it became a noted case in the movement for the abolition of slavery, gaining the involvement of such abolitionists as William Lloyd Garrison and Frederick Douglass. Eventually, with the help of a local minister, funds were raised to pay Gray four hundred dollars for the freedom of George Latimer. He began raising a family with Rebecca in nearby Chelsea. George disappeared after the Dred Scott decision, likely fearing return to slavery in the South. After his father's departure, Lewis, only nine years old at the time, had to work to help support his mother and family.

Moreover, even though slavery had been abolished in New York State, Black people were by no means considered equal to white people, and they operated on the economic fringes. Black women were forced to take on the most laborious, dull, and poorly paid work: washing, cooking, dressmaking, and sewing.

Black people were still subjected to extreme prejudice from white people in the North. Take, for example, Walt Whitman, a contemporary of Thomson's and friend of Fanny Fern's at one point, who wrote of his support for abolition, stating that slavery was "a disgrace and blot on the character of our Republic, and on our boasted humanity!"[21] But he wrote elsewhere in 1858: "Who believes that the Whites and Blacks can ever amalgamate in America? Or who wishes it to happen? Nature has set an impassable seal against it. Besides, is not America for the Whites? And is it not better so?"[22]

When the full extent of the horrors of the 1863 Draft Riots were revealed in the news, there were white people in the North who believed that the event should serve as a lesson to Black people. Maria Lydig Daly, a self-proclaimed "Union Lady" and the wife of a prominent New York City judge, wrote in her diary following the Draft Riots, "I hope it will give the Negroes a lesson, for since the war commenced, they have been so insolent as to be unbearable. I cannot endure free blacks. They are immoral, with all their piety."[23]

Even the more seemingly respected Black members of New York

society found themselves subjected to the most distressing indignities. In 1854, Elizabeth Jennings Graham had not been born free. Her father was a successful tailor and prominent member of the Black community, and her mother, Elizabeth Cartwright Jennings, was a member of the Ladies Literary Society of New York. One day, Elizabeth had climbed onto the platform of a Chatham Street horsecar on her way to church. The conductor told her to wait for the next car because "her people" were on it. When Jennings refused to step off, the conductor assaulted her and was assisted by a New York City policeman. Jennings later successfully sued the Third Avenue Railroad with the help of a plucky young attorney by the name of Chester A. Arthur, the future US president.

This lack of sympathy toward Black people, as well as an inability to see them as human or offer any kind of economic advancement, drove them to form their own communities. In New York City, Black communities were formed in Seneca Village in Manhattan (a shanty area that was later cleared to become a pocket of Central Park), Weeksville in Brooklyn, and in Queens, Newtown and a lesser-known community in Jamaica in an area known as "The Green."

While the Grommer family left few documented traces of their history, Doesticks's account of Mr. Grommer's reading is, to some degree, revealing. The Grommers did not advertise their services, preferring to stay quiet, perhaps out of a fear of what might happen to this side business should it be revealed to white people what they were doing. Once again, fortune telling seems to have offered a profession to the marginalized to practice and earn money in such a way that they could maintain autonomy. It was extraordinary that Mrs. Grommer felt empowered enough to refuse Doesticks, a white man, service; equally extraordinary is that she was able to create her own terms of service and charge a similar fee for this service as white fortune tellers. It is little wonder that such a profession offering some level of empowerment to both Black people and white women would be considered so dangerous and in need of dismantling by more "enlightened" men such as Mortimer Thomson.

What might have happened to the Grommers during the 1863 Draft Riots? Stories of atrocities committed against white abolitionists and supporters of the Black community—and mostly against the Black community— abound. Examples include a disabled child named Abraham Franklin who was hanged by a mob in front of his mother. The mob laughed at the police when they tried to interrupt the lynching. The mob later returned to mutilate Franklin's body. Jeremiah Robinson tried to escape the mob by fleeing his home dressed in his wife's clothes, but his beard gave him away, and he was captured and killed, his body flung into the river. A seven-year-old boy was forced to run from the home where he lived with his grandmother and widowed mother. Once separated from them, he was struck with cobblestones and pistols and died from his injuries.

Hopefully, the Grommers still lived in Williamsburg, where they would have been at a distance from the violence. It is estimated that by the end of the 1850s, approximately 30 percent of Brooklyn's Black population lived in Williamsburg. However, the area was not without its dangers for Black people; for example, in 1862 a Black-owned tobacco factory was attacked by whites.

Following the Draft Riots, numerous Black people fled Manhattan. By 1865, the Black population of the city had fallen by 11,000. Some Black people moved to Brooklyn. Perhaps some would find refuge with the Grommers.

Chapter 6

Mrs. Hayes

Lenormand Card: Fox (Meaning = *Untrustworthy/Deceit*)

In the eighth chapter of his book, Doesticks observed that the witches of New York promised to cure multiple diseases and, moreover, that "there are many thousands of persons who believe this stuff, and endanger their lives and health by trusting to these empirics."[1] Within two pages of the Mrs. Hayes chapter, he mentioned the grossest offender of female doctors, Madame Restell. Although Mrs. Hayes was not claiming to perform the same services as the famed abortionist, Doesticks labeled her a "dangerous and criminal" witch of the Madame Restell variety. In her advertisement cited by Doesticks, she promised "All diseases discovered and cured"— with the disclaimer "(if curable)."[2]

Upon arrival at the abode of Mrs. Hayes, Doesticks described No. 176 Grand Street as a "brick two-story dwelling, of a dingy drab color, as though it had been steeped in a Quaker atmosphere," then cringingly added that it was overlaid with "world's people's dirt." Until this point, servants had answered the doors of the fortune tellers. In this case, Doesticks was surprised to find Mrs. Hayes carrying out this drudge's task. Doesticks described her physical appearance in the most demeaning way: "She is a woman of the most abject and cringing manner imaginable; a female counterpart of Uriah Heep, with an unknown multiplication of that vermicular gentleman's writhings."[3]

Lacking in compassion for the poverty in which Mrs. Hayes was clearly living, Doesticks also compared her to a contemporary fictional character, Uriah Heep, from Charles Dickens's *Great Expectations*, which came out in serialized form in 1849 and in book form in 1850. Heep was a skinny, pallid, and cloying character, known for his insincere humility and flattery. Dickens's work had made its way to the United States and was massively popular by 1857. Dickens was even published in the same *Frank Leslie's Illustrated Weekly* as Doesticks.

The seemingly servile Mrs. Hayes invited Doesticks into the house and guided him to a chair to wait. The reception room was of "moderate size," and it afforded him views of Centre Market and the Tombs, the colloquial term for the detention center located in the Five Points neighborhood. Doesticks was also a police court reporter at the Tombs around the time he was writing *The Witches of New York*. Built in 1838 in the Egyptian Revival architectural style, it was known as a dismal place. It had been constructed on the site of the old Collect Pond, and the landfill job was shoddy, creating the most pungent and vile sanitary conditions. In 1842, Charles Dickens had written about the Tombs in his *American Notes*, stating, "Such indecent and disgusting dungeons as these cells, would bring disgrace upon the most despotic empire in the world!"[4] Doesticks rendered Mrs. Hayes's poverty and humility further with depressing sensory details of the inner room: "The crying of babies, the frizzling of cooking meat, the scraping of saucepans, and a sound of somebody scolding everybody else, predominated."[5]

Doesticks was then astounded to be greeted by *Mister* Hayes. For the first and only time, a man would oversee the financial transactions of a woman's fortune telling business. Doesticks's description of Mr. Hayes was even less flattering than his description of his wife. Doesticks wrote that "he was surrounded by an atmosphere of fried onions, and the fragrant and greasy perspiration in his face seemed to have been distilled from that favorite vegetable." Like Uriah Heep, Mr. Hayes was tall and thin, but he had a fierce and rough demeanor, with a cockney accent that had "harsh tones" and "the threatenings of an ill-natured bull-dog."[6]

Mr. Hayes advised Doesticks that there were plenty of con artist clairvoyants around town who pretended to cure the sick, but he and Mrs. Hayes were the real deal. They only offered Mrs. Hayes's authentic, medically intuitive advice for the good of society. Among her many talents, Mrs. Hayes could tell Doesticks whether he or his wife was well or sick, and they could get in touch with absent friends, but they could not resolve any arguments or difficulties he might be having with his spouse.

Doesticks expressed to Mr. Hayes that he didn't have a wife and that he was simply inquiring after the well-being of friends in Minnesota, so he could obtain peace of mind. At that, Mr. Hayes commanded his wife to come back into the room to see Doesticks. Mrs. Hayes shuffled obediently into the room and sat herself down on an armchair, where she began to twitch and contort her face into a variety of expressions, from inane smiles to mouth jerks, finally settling on a passive countenance. During this process, Mr. Hayes drew down the window shades, veiling the room in darkness.

Mrs. Hayes began to speak, telling Doesticks to go with an unnamed gentleman to Brooklyn and follow wherever this man told him to go. Then Mrs. Hayes's voice became baby-like and whining. In this voice, she told Doesticks he must cross water in a boat. Then he would get in a yellow car, arriving at a brick house with green blinds. No, it was a wood house with green blinds and carpet and chairs. She could see a pretty, young lady with blue eyes and an elderly lady. They also appeared to be going on a journey on a boat. They were then at a railroad with a pretty baby. Then they traveled past a river and a mill and a pretty cow, past a pretty little carriage and a pretty dog. By this time (probably having become tired of the adjective "pretty"), she said the travelers would reach St. Paul, which she described as having two colleges, a city hall built of white marble, a locomotive factory, and a place where they were building seven ocean steamers. They would then arrive at a house. Doesticks began to press Mrs. Hayes for more information. But she seemed unable to provide specific answers to his questions. Instead, she described a certain area of Minnesota, stating it was a small town located "911 miles southeast of the mouth of the Mississippi" (this makes no sense geographically), along with some other trivia about the area.

Perplexed and feeling he had heard quite enough, Doesticks summoned Mr. Hayes back into the room; gave him the hand of Mrs. Hayes, whom he described as a "twaddling adult baby"; and paid Mr. Hayes *his* dollar. As Mr. Hayes pulled Mrs. Hayes out of her trance, Doesticks observed: "She didn't seem glad to get her soul back again."[7] Perhaps she was not eager to return to the world of her rough, domineering husband, screaming children, and fried onions. The mystical was a place where she could disappear and imagine open skies, fresh air, and small, well-kept towns, a place where a woman could breathe deeply and escape the challenges of impoverished city living.

With the onset of the Civil War, "absent friends" came to be at the forefront of Thomson's mind. He signed up to serve and commenced work as a war correspondent, but his role would later change in peculiar ways. The war meant he and Grace would spend little time together during their marriage, though they had come to know each other somewhat well before the ceremony.

That year, he wrote an article titled "Doesticks Respectfully Inquireth: What Do the Women Want Us to Do about the War?" In his opening, he wrote, "One reason why it is so difficult to please a woman is, that she seldom knows herself what she wants."[8] He complained that his wife seemed to be of two minds regarding the war. If a man did not sign up, she would sulk and accuse him of being a coward. If he did, she would mock his uniform but then run over to her neighbor to brag about how splendid her husband looked. When the day came that her husband was to leave, she said she would never speak to him again as she just knew he would be killed. Considering that the Doesticks articles are written in a humorous vein and subject to exaggeration, it is hard to tell whether Grace truly expressed these conflicting feelings.

On October 3, 1861, the *Cass County Republican* reported that Thomson was temporarily acting as chaplain of the New York Twenty-Sixth Volunteers, Col. Christian. The newspaper stated that he was unexpectedly called upon to perform that duty until a trained chaplain could be found. There is no information regarding why Thomson was selected; perhaps it was because of his background in public speaking.

Fifty years later, a curious report appeared in the *Brooklyn Daily Eagle*. General Newtown Martin Curtis, a Civil War hero, gave a speech in Ithaca for Oneida County's veterans. He recollected an incident in northeastern Virginia when he found soldiers of the Twenty-Sixth regiment, the Second Oneida regiment, intoxicated. "It was the rule," General Curtis stated, "to give the members of all fatigue parties a half gill of whisky per man when called off for dinner." General Curtis decided the men had had enough and cut them off from their rations. Later, he was approached by a man protesting the denial of his daily dose of whiskey. The man told him, "I am an officer, one not required to supervise men at drill or labor, but to guard them from evil influences and bad associations. I am the chaplain of the Twenty-sixth New York."[9] That man then further revealed himself to be the reporter Mortimer Thomson, writing under the pseudonym of Q. K. Philander Doesticks, P.B. General Curtis concluded his story by stating he had yet to find the name of Doesticks or Mortimer Thomson on the roster of the Twenty-Sixth. It is not clear why that would be, as Thomson's role was confirmed in newspaper accounts.

Thomson's prankish behavior continued even during the somberness of the Civil War. In 1861, Gunn had pasted in his diary a jovial account written by Thomson titled "Doesticks' First Night of Soldiering":

> The first two hours' drill of a raw recruit must be excruciatingly funny to the disinterested observer. My own experience is as follows:
>
> Up five flights of stairs, as narrow and as crooked as if the maker had contracted to build a circular stairway inside a chimney and had done it. Into a large room at the very top of the house. In fact, our drill-room is so high up, that in case of a thunder-shower, we have clear sky up there before the first drops of the rain reach the ground. It takes so long to get up stairs, that Haney always takes a lunch to eat when he gets half-way up, and always smokes nineteen pipes to refresh himself before he enters on his evening's arduous duties of criticizing the recruits, and making bad jokes about the awkward squad. Haney has measured the distance from the sidewalk to the drill-room, and finds that it is four cigars, six clay-pipes, and a meerschaum and a half. . . .
>
> When you go for the first time to drill, your drill-officer proceeds upon the supposition that you don't know anything at all, and, as a general thing, drill officer is about right: so he first teaches you to stand, to walk, and to turn around. Officer told me how to stand in the "position of a soldier"—listened carefully—thought I understood it—but I saw so many grins on the faces of the spectators, that in two minutes I didn't know whether he had told me to "turn out" my feet or my eyes; whether to "project my stomach" out before or behind; whether my eyes or my chin was to "strike the ground at the distance of fifteen paces;" and couldn't tell whether my head or my heels were to be "square to the front." Tried to do as the rest did, for the present, but resolved to pay off all the grinners in the future—when I get to be a General. . . .
>
> After a few more trials, things went a little better, and we can now go through all our squad drills, without risk of walking through the windows—without endangering the lives of bystanders—without tearing our clothes, and without getting so mad that the officers have to lock up the muskets.[10]

In addition to his buffoonery, Thomson seems to have been absent-minded, losing valuable possessions in the early days of the war. In September 1861, several ads appeared in newspapers, offering a five-dollar reward for the return of a Colt's seven-inch revolver, silver mounted, with the inscription "Mortimer Thomson, 1861." It was requested to return the

Mortimer Thomson, 1862, from Thomas Butler Gunn's Diaries, Vol. 22, Missouri Historical Society Archives, St. Louis.

Mortimer Thomson, Smith College Special Collections.

A POPULAR LECTURER AND AUTHOR.—DOESTICKS.

Cartoon image of Mortimer Thomson by Thomas Butler Gunn, Missouri Historical Society Archives, St. Louis.

Doesticks takes the whole World to his Bosom, including his Creditors.

Cartoon image of Mortimer Thomson in *Frank Leslie's Illustrated Newspaper*, 1860 (from the author's collection).

THE

WITCHES OF NEW YORK.

A FAITHFUL

Revelation and Exposition of the Doings

OF ALL

THE PRINCIPAL ASTROLOGISTS, SORCERESSES, PROPHETS, CLAIRVOYANTS, WITCHES, PLANET READERS, AND OTHER VOTARIES OF THE BLACK ART IN THE CITY OF NEW YORK.

BY

Q. K. PHILANDER DOESTICKS, P.B.

AUTHOR OF "DOESTICKS' LETTERS," "THE ELEPHANT CLUB," "PLU-RI-BUS-TAH," ETC., ETC.

"Doesticks is one of the few immortal names that were not born to die. Doesticks will always be with us. We have only to step into our library, and behold, there is the ubiquitous Doesticks! We take him by the hand—we listen to the thoughts that breathe—the quaint philosophy—the piquant illustrations! Doesticks all over—Doesticks in every page—in every line! Do you wish to make the acquaintance of Doesticks? Every body does."—*New York Railway Journal*.
"Doesticks' is irresistibly funny."—*P. T. Barnum's Letter to the N. Y. Tribune*.

Philadelphia:

T. B. PETERSON AND BROTHERS,
306 CHESTNUT STREET..

Frontispiece, *The Witches of New York* by Q.K. Philander Doesticks, P.B., first edition, 1858 (from the author's collection).

Cartoon image in *The Witches of New York* by Q.K. Philander Doesticks, P.B., first edition, 1858 (from the author's collection).

Mortimer Thomson tombstone, Green-Wood Cemetery, Brooklyn, New York (photo by the author).

Tribune Office.

New York. Oct 4. 1860.

My dear Madam -

I owe you an apology
for my long delay in
complying with your
request - here it is.

Your letter reached
here when I was absent,
and has been mislaid

First page of letter from Mortimer Thomson,
1860 (from the author's collection).

all these weeks. I make
the only reparation I can,
by sending you at last
the autograph you desire,
and entreating you to
remember that it is
" better late, than never."

Yours very Truly.

Mortimer Thomson.

Second page of letter from Mortimer Thomson,
1860 (from the author's collection).

Grace Eldredge, Smith College Special Collections.

Fanny Fern, Smith College Special Collections.

Fanny Fern tombstone, Mount Auburn Cemetery, Cambridge, Massachusetts (photo by the author).

Ethel and Mark Thomson (Mortimer Thomson's children), Newburyport Public Library Archival Center.

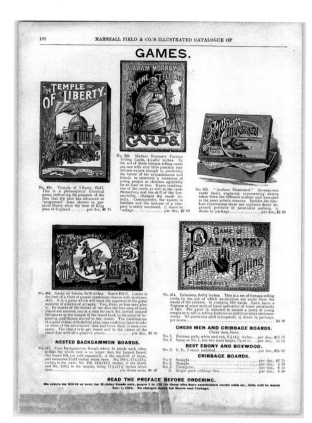

Marshall Field & Co.'s Illustrated
Catalogue of Games listing Madam
Morrow's Fortune Telling Cards, 1894.

"Dens of Death" by Jacob Riis, 1872.

"Mulberry Bend" by Jacob Riis, 1890.

"Sewing Pants for the 'Sweater' in a Gotham Court 'Flat'" by Jacob Riis, 1890.

revolver to Mortimer Thomson, who was staying at 251 F Street, between Thirteenth and Fourteenth, in Washington, DC, at the time, or to Mr. Chadwick at Willard's Hotel. Moreover, on November 21, 1861, Thomson's more responsible younger brother Clifford placed an advertisement under "Miscellaneous" in the *Local News* in Alexandria, Virginia. The ad offered a five-dollar reward for the return of a waterproof cloak or cape marked on the inside with the name "Mortimer Thomson, November 1861."[11] The item was to be returned to Clifford. Since the ad was taken out on November 21, 1861, and the cloak bore the date of that very month, it could not have been in Thomson's possession for very long before he lost it.

However, Thomson did appear to have one moment of heroism at the start of the Civil War. One newspaper account reported that he had traveled alone to New York from the lower Chesapeake Bay to appeal for assistance to one of the disastrously placed regiments. According to the article, this task had "required indomitable pluck for its fulfillment."[12]

Thomson's brother Clifford appeared to take his role during the war much more seriously. Born in Fulton, New York, in 1834, not too far from Mortimer's place of birth, Clifford had initially worked as a journeyman printer, performing the general maintenance of printing presses and cleaning the press room, as well as mixing inks and solvents. Journeymen printers did not need to work under supervision, meaning they could move from job to job and from shop to shop without need for guidance. At twenty-two, Clifford fell ill and decided to recover by living among Native Americans in Minnesota for several years. He then prospected for gold in California. When President Lincoln issued a proclamation on April 15, 1861, calling for 75,000 volunteer militiamen, Clifford enrolled as a private in the Lincoln Cavalry, which subsequently became the First New York Cavalry.

At the Battle of Chancellorsville in 1863, Clifford rendered special service, for which he was awarded the Congressional Medal of Honor. His citation read: "This officer volunteered to ascertain the character of the approaching troops, rode up so closely as to distinguish the features of the enemy, and as he wheeled to return, they opened fire with musketry, the Union troops returning same. Under a terrific fire from both sides Lieutenant Thomson rode back unhurt to the Federal lines, averting a terrible disaster to the army by his heroic act."[13]

By the close of the Civil War, Clifford had been appointed a major of the Fifth United States Volunteer Colored Cavalry. When the war began, Lincoln had decided that Black people could only be used as laborers, not combat soldiers. However, by the end of 1862, it appeared the war was not going to end any time soon, and the number of northern white volunteers had dropped considerably. Lincoln issued the Emancipation Proclamation on January 1, 1863. Not only did this liberate slaves in areas still in rebellion, but it also allowed freed Black men to serve in combat in the armed forces. However, it was a common attitude among white abolitionists at the time that even though they agreed Black people should be freed from slavery, they were still not considered equal to whites. Therefore, Black cavalries were commanded by white men. Thus Clifford's appointment.

Thomson did not rise in the ranks the same way as his brother. On February 11, 1862, the *Buffalo Commercial* mentioned that he had prepared a new poetic lecture titled "The War—a Huge Joke."[14] If that lecture's title accurately foretold its contents, it conflicted with his "Pluck" lectures, which he continued to deliver on a regular basis during the rest of the war.

Thomson would have occasional leave, including in October 1861, when Gunn reported Thomson had briefly returned from Virginia because of diarrhea. In the nineteenth century, diarrhea was quite serious. The idiom "no guts, no glory" originated with US Civil War troops, who decided on a rule that men should not be shot at while answering the call of nature. The prevalence of diarrhea was so strong and problematic in the 1800s that the expression that a man "had to have guts" to fight as a soldier became common. Thomson was once again dispatched to the south by the *Tribune* but returned in mid-November. Gunn reported that their mutual friend Frank Cahill (also coauthor of *The Magician's Own Book*) said that Thomson was so ill and worn as to look ghastly. "His face is thin and hollow, with deep, black, ominous shades round the eyes."[15] Cahill, who theorized that Thomson was overworked and excited, predicted that he would not live six more months.

According to Gunn, Thomson was disgraced and arrested at Port Royal to such a degree that he lost his position at the *Tribune*. Gunn felt it was perhaps a muddled story and believed Thomson lost his job because he was a costly employee. Before Thomson had even gone to war as a correspondent, he had expensed a couple of hundred dollars for an outfit, purchasing revolvers and field glasses. At first, the *Tribune* suggested he might make more money than his journalist's salary if he lectured. However, Thomson didn't take the hint, and so they had to discharge him.

Thomson continued to pen some tongue-in-cheek articles about marriage. In the *Saturday Evening Post*, he published an article titled "What Doesticks' Wife Wanted." In the opening of the article, Doesticks and his wife were taking a stroll down Broadway, the shopping mecca, and noted that his wife "wants everything she sees, and the consequences can only be computed." Doesticks supposed his wife thought him a millionaire, as the article detailed the many things his wife saw that she wanted to purchase, including a carriage for $1,400, a buggy for $270, a piano for $375, a harp for $200, a Newfoundland dog for $50, four hundred dresses averaging $50 each, and so forth. The article grew increasingly absurd as his wife urged him to buy "one gun . . . for the baby, one dollar."[16] The article concluded with Doesticks humorously begging merchants to keep their goods in their house instead of tempting him and his wife into coveting all of them.

Shortly after this article came out, Grace took a tumble down the stairs, hurting herself. It was a worrisome bout of clumsiness because she was pregnant. Parton had apparently demonstrated little sympathy over this incident, calling Grace, as Gunn reported, "the most vacant-minded, inane of young women, preferring her younger sister, the (to me and everybody else) highly-objectionable Nelly." Gunn defined Thomson's second marriage as a "Dead Sea apple . . . all of them reaping as they sowed, and the poor girl lying under the clods in Green-Wood is avenged. Grace and Fanny hate Mrs. Thomson; Mort is away with Cliff in Virginia working hard and sadly to keep the double family and, in Haney's words, the punishment falls hardest on the one who had nothing to do with the match— Mort's Father. Grace gets her income and spends it."[17]

His remarks about Grace and Fanny hating Thomson's mother seem oddly harsh, particularly given that they had all been good friends. However, Gunn had recently had a falling out with Fanny Fern. In 1859, while Thomson was wooing Grace, Gunn had written a satirical article about the *New York Ledger* in the magazine *Scalpel*. Gunn attacked the paper because he had approached its editor, Robert Bonner, who had rejected every single one of his ideas. Fern was livid, as her personal loyalties were naturally with her publication. It had helped establish her career, and she was still its top writer. Gunn was now no longer welcome in her home, and Thomson appeared less frequently in his diaries, except for accounts of professional and casual encounters. Any mentions of Fern in Gunn's diaries afterward are nasty.

Gunn received through his gossip grapevine the news that Thomson and his wife had three servants (that would explain why Thomson was so disdainful of the dirt and clutter of the tenements; he had no experience of cleaning up after himself) and that Grace would pose on the sofa, watching passersby like a heroine in a novel. Chin-wagging neighbors said that Thomson would also strut up and down in front of the house in the morning in a fancy dressing gown with a newspaper and talking to Grace through an open window.

On September 24, 1862, Gunn met Thomson's father, Edwin, for the first time, accidentally bumping into him at the *Tribune* office. Gunn described the father as "middle-aged, spare, grave-looking . . . with rather a big stick."[18] He had come to the office with a letter from Clifford, who had recently been appointed aide to General Pleasanton. Gunn also reported that, like Thomson, his father was a drunkard. "It was this vice that caused his alienation from his family and his absence in California." This is perhaps why there is little mention of Thomson's father in family documents. In his journal entry for that week, Gunn was not kind about Thomson, either. "Everyway Doesticks develops as a selfish humbug, a spendthrift, a blackguard and a profligate. He tried to bully papa on behalf of Fanny."[19] It seems Thomson had gone to collect money from a mutual friend that was borrowed from Fanny Fern, who—according to Gunn—would never let any debt rest, including one owed Parton by Walt Whitman.

By October, Grace was heavily pregnant and not faring well. "Dixon tells me that Mort Thomson's wife is enceinte and that Mort wants him to attend her. The doctor thinks it wouldn't pay."[20] Around the same time, Gunn had pasted into his diary a photograph of Thomson looking bohemian and dapper.[21] He wore a beret and a well-groomed moustache, bow-tie, vest, and overcoat. He looked well fitted and handsomely tailored, as though he had just been on a spending spree. The cost of a portrait may also have set him back. The price of ambrotypes and tintypes ranged from twenty-five cents to $2.50 in the United States in that era (in 2023, that's eight to seventy-five dollars). Gunn also learned that Thomson had spent a thousand dollars of Grace's money to pay off debts he had accumulated before he was married to her. Fanny Fern became enraged when she heard about it.

As the country became more deeply entrenched in the war, Thomson's sanity seemed to leave him. Gunn wrote, "Mort had delirium tremens and was about to throw himself into the river, once; when he was saved by the butcher from whose shop he had rushed to the dock side."[22]

On December 1, 1862, Grace gave birth to their first child, Ethel. However, she became ill shortly after, having contracted scarlet fever from Mark Thomson, who was staying with Grace at the time. She wasn't aware that he was sick and had brought Mark into her bedroom to see the baby.

Grace passed away on December 13, 1862, but her death is not mentioned in Gunn's diary until February 5, 1863; he seemed much less moved by Grace's death than by that of Chips. In his diary, Gunn wrote that Thomson had apparently wished to leave Ethel with Fern for only a few years, or at least until the war was over. Fern wished for Ethel to remain with her and Parton indefinitely. Moreover, while Grace's estate was being settled, it was discovered that Thomson had spent all but $1,500 of

Grace's inheritance from her grandfather. That meant he had spent $5,500 ($167,000+ in 2023) within a year and a half. Fern wanted Thomson to leave what little money remained to Ethel, but Thomson wanted to use it to study medicine. "Here's a precious fellow!"[23] Gunn remarked.

More tales of drama ensued in the Gunn diary two months later. Grace's sister Ellen professed to despise Thomson, who was at that point studying to become an army surgeon. Gunn wrote, "He lied, grossly, to account for his apparent command of means, saying that his salary had been raised, and what not. The fellow is utterly, irreclaimably base and selfish. Fanny has gushed in the Ledger, of course, about Grace's death, and about the baby, the dear old ghoule and cannibal that she is."[24]

The article to which Gunn alluded is perhaps Fern's article "An Offer," in which she ranted about the hypocrisies of men in seeking a wife. "Tom Jones would like to be married. Tom does not quite relish the idea of a connubial idiot; and yet, for many reasons unnecessary to state, he does not desire a wife who knows much. . . . He would like her always to be very nicely dressed, although his own attire is slovenly." The final clincher of the opinion piece is almost certainly a dig at Thomson's financial opportunism in marrying Grace. "Any young lady very weak in the head, and strong in the nerves, and quite destitute of any disgusting little selfishness, may consider herself eligible, provided she has money."[25]

Gunn ranted more, accusing Thomson of astounding carelessness while Grace was sick. When she was hot and feverish, Thomson lifted her out of bed and put her on a settee beside an open window in December. Perhaps, Gunn pondered, Thomson had been trying to kill her after Grace realized he was squandering her money. Gunn had also speculated that Thomson was drunk while attending his dying first wife, which, given how Thomson's life was about to play out, does not seem such a far-fetched speculation.

Mrs. Hayes seems also to have found herself in an unfortunate marriage. In 1851, an article appeared in the *New York Daily Herald* regarding the sudden death of Mrs. Eliza Ann Austin, who was living with her husband on Second Street in Manhattan. As the newspaper reported, her death was caused by the malpractice of Dr. George Hays (the reporters seem to have spelled the Hayes's last names incorrectly and inconsistently), a self-proclaimed clairvoyant physician at 116 Spring Street.[26]

Several weeks earlier, Mrs. Austin had been seized by an attack of inflammation of the lungs, and Dr. Belcher, "a respectable physician," was called upon. Under his care, Mrs. Austin appeared to make improvements but continued to be troubled by a cough. "Dr. Hayes" was recommended to Mrs. Austin by a friend, and she began consulting this self-professed doctor. He put his wife, Mrs. Hayes, in a trance, and she told Mrs. Austin that she had inflammation in the lungs and must apply leeches for blood-letting, as well as a carrot poultice and cough mixture. The practice of using leeches may seem highly suspect to our contemporary sensibility, but professional physicians in the 1850s were still using them, and in fact, leeches are still used in microsurgery today.

Mrs. Austin had followed the advice of Mrs. Hayes, but twenty hours after the commencement of the treatment she began to rapidly decline, and she died the following day. Mrs. Austin was examined by a Dr. Franklin, who found the lining of her stomach to be highly inflamed and softened, with the traces of a poisonous liquid lodged in the stomach. Both lungs were congested.

Dr. Hayes and his wife were arrested and taken to the Tombs during the investigation. The media does not seem to have followed the outcome of this trial, but clearly the couple was released not too long after. In less than a year, Dr. and Mrs. Hayes were again advertising their services in the newspapers, and Mrs. Hayes was one of the subjects of an investigative article written in the same year.

On November 23, 1855, three years before Thomson wrote his articles, a reporter for the New York Times (no name attached, as the practice of bylines was not widespread in 1855) decided to venture out to visit the clairvoyants of New York City with his friend "Damon." Unlike Doesticks, this reporter described himself as not skeptical, claiming to have always had an interest in the stars. The first clairvoyant the reporter and Damon chose to visit was Mrs. Hayes.

The Times reporter was much kinder in his assessment of Mrs. Hayes's environs, stating that No. 176 Grand Street was a "tenement of humble, but respectable appearance. Labels on the hall door announce the existence of a Doctor Hayes, whom it is charitable to suppose is the husband of our clairvoyante, and a professional looking basement favors the supposition that the Doctor, in some dubious manner, practices the medical professional [sic]."[27] The reporter further attested to finding the area plain and prosaic.

With his friend at his side, the reporter rang the bell, confessing that he expected the door to open on its own accord or that they would be greeted by a dwarf with golden anklets and a long feather in his cap. However, to their disappointment, the door was opened plainly by a woman. The men first inquired after Dr. Hayes, but finding he was not at home, they asked for Mrs. Hayes. The woman answered that she was Mrs. Hayes. She invited the gentlemen in and ushered them up to the back room of the second floor. There, the reporter observed that the apartment functioned as a kitchen, laundry, and bedroom. A baby slept in a bed in a corner of the room. There were gleaming pots and saucepans, as well as a couple of flatirons heating. The reporter wrote he was disappointed to find the room so ordinary, with no mystical or exotic-looking objects.

Like Doesticks, this author wrote sneeringly of the appearance of Mrs. Hayes, whom he described as looking to be about forty and having a complexion "the texture of second quality lard."[28] Mrs. Hayes explained that she had showed the gentlemen into her sleeping quarters because the reception room didn't have a fire.

The reporter's friend, Damon, although apparently healthy, invented a vague disease for which he hoped to find a cure. The reporter sat on a hard chair and conversed with Mrs. Hayes. He asked her if she had many patients. Mrs. Hayes said she had many but that they tired her out. The reporter asked how she came to discover her power as a clairvoyant. Mrs. Hayes stated that she was troubled by a swollen hand when she was a young girl. Initially, she had gone to a Doctor Mott, who told her that her hand should be cut off. Melancholy at this prospect, Mrs. Hayes visited "an electric doctor," Doctor Brown, who magnetized her. This made her condition worse. She resolved to have her hand cut off by Doctor Mott, but her brother urged her to try Doctor Brown one more time. This time the doctor asked her under hypnosis what could cure her hand. Mrs. Hayes answered raw clams. She followed this treatment plan and was shortly after cured of her problem. Mrs. Hayes had since been inspired to help others.

Damon inquired whether Mrs. Hayes would ever intuit how to find lost property, for large sums of money were offered to those with such skills, but Mrs. Hayes seemed to balk at the prospect of money. Damon also asked if Mrs. Hayes knew of Madame Morrow, who professed to tell everything. Mrs. Hayes said she had heard of her but then mentioned that she shouldn't like to know as much as Madame Morrow and that she was honest about her limitations.

Damon then asked Mrs. Hayes's age. After he guessed with false flattery that she was twenty-two, Mrs. Hayes replied that she was thirty-seven (this was likely true, as she was reported in the newspapers in 1858 as being forty). Doctor Hayes entered the room, making a similar impression on the reporter as he had on Doesticks. This reporter declared, "I never beheld a more villainous looking person. Had I met him at a sea-port in France, I should have called the Police and made him strip."[29]

The two reporters were swiftly guided by Doctor Hayes into the front parlor, where he lit two yellow tallow candles. Mrs. Hayes was conducted to a rocking chair, and Doctor Hayes proceeded to mesmerize Mrs. Hayes. Doctor Hayes told the reporter to take off his glove and place his hand into the hand of Mrs. Hayes. Mrs. Hayes began to speak, initially in gibberish, but then with clarity:

> *Seeress*—I am in this gentlemen's head, but I see nothing there, (*Damon winces*); there seems to be nothing the matter with his head. He is nervous, and at times the blood presses on that portion where the deltoid joins the cerebellum. Then he has a pain and feels bad, (*pause.*) There is nothing the matter with his troth, (*throat*). I look in his chist [*sic*] and I can't see anything bad there. I look for ulcers on the lungs, but cannot see any—(*pause*)—no! I cannot see any ulcerations.[30]

Mrs. Hayes continued in this way for each body part, eventually noting that the pericardium pressed on the abdomen and that the orifice of the diaphragm was inflamed. She said that Damon tended to hide his pain from his friends. Damon asked for a cure, and Mrs. Hayes offered that a nice sherry wine accompanied by a cent and a half's worth of yellow dock root, wild cherry bark, and chamomile flowers, taken in a glass every day before dinner, should do the trick. She also recommended a lotion of alcohol mixed with three parts water and a pinch of salt, mixed in a bottle, and that Damon should dip his hand in it now and then and rub it over the lower part of his abdomen.

The reporter wanted to test Mrs. Hayes's powers further, to see if she could, as claimed, read his mind. He asked her to go with him to Liverpool and then the southwestern coast of Ireland. At each place, he asked her to describe the features of each place. The reporter was utterly disgusted by the inaccuracies and vagueness of her descriptions. Having had enough, he requested that Mrs. Hayes be awoken, which she was. Nonetheless, he paid his two dollars to Dr. Hayes, who apologized for the disappointment. The reporter concluded his visit to Mrs. Hayes with this summary:

> So much for clairvoyance in New-York. There are probably one hundred of these people existing in various parts of the city on the credulity of fools, and greenhorns from the country. They profess to tell everything, and tell nothing. The uneducated mind is easily

deceived by any affectation of mystery, and the vagueness of Mrs. Hayes' replies would, on persons unaccustomed to investigation, create a powerful effect. That she was not asleep I am convinced, and were it not that her husband was very big and strong, and my feelings of gallantry deeply seated, I think I would have stuck a pin in her to test the reality of the *coma*.[31]

This *Times* report did not seem to embarrass or deter Mrs. Hayes, if she had read the article or been made aware of it at all. A year later, in the *New York Daily Herald* on June 12, 1856, Mrs. Hayes placed an advertisement claiming to cure everything from deafness, lameness, and rheumatism to nervous diseases, asthma, and bronchitis. Similar ads could be found in 1857 in the *New York Daily Herald* and *Arkansas Intelligencer*. In 1859, she grandly claimed, "Paralysis cured at once." Since 1852, her advertisements often mentioned the services of her husband, Dr. Hayes. His title was frequently "electrician and psychologist" ("electrician" meant a worker in electromagnetism). After 1856, Dr. Hayes appeared in no more advertisements with Mrs. Hayes. Perhaps he had died. Perhaps he simply went missing, like so many husbands did in that era. He could also have decided to keep a lower profile.

In October 1858, several newspapers reported that the mayor's squad had made twelve arrests, exposing humbugs who had been the subjects of numerous complaints. The arrest spree had included Mrs. Harris, the "Gipsy palmist," Mrs. Wilson, Madame Lane, Mary Roe, Madame Jason, Madame Widger, Mrs. Carst, Madame Prewster, A. W. Snow, Madame York, and Madame Fleury. Mrs. Hayes was also among the arrests at her home at 327 Broome Street. Instead of being mesmerized by her husband, it was stated that she was put in a trance by a servant who took hold of her hand but was jolted awake by the announcement of the police. After being arrested by Sergeant Croft, Mrs. Hayes was placed under the protection of one Officer Place.

Mrs. Hayes continued to be undeterred, placing ads for her services in the newspapers. Normally her advertisements did not name a fee, but her 1862 ad for her abode at 36 Leroy Street stated a charge of one dollar, half the amount she was charging in 1855. The last traceable ad for her clairvoyant services appeared on May 26, 1863, when she promised to cure "rheumatism and all nervous diseases."

Why were Thomson and the *Times* reporter so intent on framing these "witches," who were making far less money than the likes of the corrupt mayor Boss Tweed? The concept of the witch has shape-shifted over time, but throughout history, those who have been defined as witches are often women or those who are women-identified who want or already are in a position of economic, social, or political power. Until the 1960s and 1970s, "witch" was an identity mostly forced upon someone, as it often follows some kind of societal persecution. As so-called witches upset the patriarchal order, there are often some male characters skulking in the background, scheming over ways to bring these "witches" down.

Take, for example, the history of alewives. From the earliest evidence of brewing in 7000 BCE until the commercialization of brewing during industrialization, women were the primary brewers on all inhabited continents. In medieval times, an alewife would identify her status as a brewer of beer by placing a broom outside her house. She wore a pointy black hat for easy identification in public houses. She brewed potions in large cauldrons. She kept cats for pest control. One immediately notices the associations of the symbolism. Women were making excellent money in this profession, and as has often been documented throughout history, most men don't like it when women prosper economically and maintain autonomy over their finances. Men began to encourage society to persecute these alewives with accusations of witchcraft.

Across the sixteenth and seventeenth centuries, brewing in Europe changed from being a women's profession to one dominated by men, although women were still involved in the sale of beer. From the middle of the eighteenth century, many women were barred from participating in alcohol production and were relegated to roles as barmaids, pub operators, bottlers, or secretaries at breweries. In less industrialized areas, they continued to produce homebrews and traditional alcoholic beverages.

Could it be that Thomson was appalled on a subconscious level by these women earning their own money, stating their terms, and controlling their careers? History suggests that this well could have been a factor, and in fact, Thomson himself had benefited from his society's enforcement of the economic dependence of women, taking advantage of his significantly wealthier second wife once all her money legally became his.

Chapter 7

The Gipsy Girl

Lenormand Card: Mice (Meaning = *Stress, Deterioration*)

Of all the chapters in Doesticks's *The Witches of New York*, "The Gipsy Girl" was the saddest, hardly the Meg Merrilies of Sir Walter Scott's *Guy Mannering* and John Keats's eponymous poem.[1] Most of the women Doesticks investigated named themselves *Madame* This or *Mrs.* That, but this fortune teller simply called herself "The Gipsy Girl." On occasion she would also use the names "The Gipsy Woman," "The Gipsy Palmist," and "The Gipsy Wonder."[2]

Despite these mysterious and fantastical names, Doesticks believed this fortune teller had not been successful in making money, perhaps because she lacked connections. She also had a "fondness for gin" and was notorious for delivering driveled, drunken fortunes. The journalist claimed he could write an entire chapter dedicated to those ramblings. He wrote that he visited her three times, so peculiar were her readings.

Before exiting for his visit, Doesticks stated that he would leave his watch and pocketbook at home, insinuating that either one might be stolen by this gipsy. All he brought with him was the small change needed to pay her for her services. She charged fifty cents, half of what most fortune tellers were compensated. This seems to foreshadow the poverty in which Doesticks would find his subject living.

Approaching the Gipsy Girl's block, Doesticks observed a squat building, three stories high, with a "sickly smoke" issuing from the chimney. The door was answered by a little girl whom Doesticks described as "ragged," as well as "saucy and dirty-faced."[3] She was whip smart, though, he thought, because she could smell his fifty cents and invited him upstairs with a skip and a twirl, showing Doesticks into the reception room with a flourish, then disappearing from sight. While waiting, he observed a threadbare carpet and an ill-lit stove, producing little heat. There was a shabby sofa and a lounge with a tattered cover, through which "suspicious" bits of curled hair poked out and suggested to Doesticks there might be cockroaches and other insects setting up home in the furniture. There were three shaky chairs set up and a "grim skeleton" of a table.

Doesticks heard glasses clinking in an adjacent apartment, and then the Gipsy Girl made her appearance. "She is of medium height, her eyes are brown and bright, and her hands are very large and red," Doesticks wrote of her:

> She has no hair, but wears a scratch red wig, which gives her head a utilitarian character. Her face is deeply pitted with the small-pox, more than pitted—gullied, scarred, and seamed, as though some jealous rival had been trying to plough her complexion under. . . . Her nails were horny and ill-shaped, and underneath them and at their roots were large deposits of dirt and other fertilizing compounds, under the stimulating influence of which they had grown lank and long.

This alarming appearance was accompanied by the strong scent of gin wafting from the Gipsy Girl, who drew up a chair to the table where Doesticks sat, "as if she had been dumped from a cart."[4] She commanded her fifty cents, and after Doesticks gave her his change, she took his left hand and examined it for a minute.

She attempted to state that he was a person who had seen great difficulty but stumbled over her words, losing her breath. She faltered again over an assortment of words that Doesticks transcribed as *diffleculency*, *diffle*, and *difflety*, before settling on *difflety*. After struggling with the word *difficulty*, her fluency appeared to pick up, yet her statements were hackneyed and repetitive. If he had been a luckier man in his past life, she told him, he would not have had so much *difflety* and strife. He would also see much *difflety* and trouble in the future, becoming sick, though he would live to be sixty-nine years of age. He would have money, plenty of money. An *Hinglish* relative would leave him money during middle *hage*. He would have to cross the *hocean* to get the money, but the money would leave him *'appy* for the rest of his days. He would thrive in business. He would not have troubles. He would never see sickness. He would have many friends.

At this point, the Gipsy Girl seemed to have utterly forgotten her initial thread. Doesticks was to have one wife, and in three months, he would hear from her by letter, and in the fourth month, he would be married. This wife would not be particularly handsome or *hugly*. Completely tossing away her script, the Gipsy Girl proclaimed the future Doesticks to be the happiest man in all the land. He would have three children with his first wife and would see no *difflety* and trouble. He would die in a foreign land across the ocean a happy man.

"Romance and poesy were effectually demolished by the overpowering realities of dirt, vulgarity, cockneyism, ignorance, scratch-wigs, bad English, and bad gin,"[5] he concluded. Doesticks was escorted down the stairs by the delightful yet shabby young girl who had initially greeted him. Above, he could hear the clink of a bottle and glass emanating from the home of the Gipsy Girl, who seemed to have returned to her "devotions."

Thomson's downward spiral following the death of his two wives in some ways closely mimics that of the Gipsy Girl. Contrary to what she predicted, Thomson was to struggle with the same sickness as she did in his last days.

He remained a bachelor following the death of Grace. One cannot help but wonder, given the continual hints in his writing that the fortune tellers were practicing or former prostitutes and his seemingly familiar knowledge of brothels, whether Thomson might have frequented these houses of ill repute, especially in his widowed years. His daughter, Ethel Parton, once wrote that Thomson's "Bohemian manner of life was not suited to my rearing as a little girl."[6]

Thomson's travels on the lecture circuit could also have made him an unsuitable parent to Ethel. In 1862, the *Quad City Times* in Davenport, Iowa, announced that Henry Ward Beecher would be a speaker at a course of lectures for the Young Men's Association at Metropolitan Hall. Among the other speakers were Ralph Waldo Emerson, Horace Greeley, and Mortimer Thomson, alias Doesticks, delivering his "Pluck" lecture.[7]

Sometimes, Thomson's newspaper assignments would take him out of the country. In 1863, for example, Thomson visited Liverpool, England, to hear Henry Ward Beecher speak in front of a "howling mob of 4,000." In the *Democrat and Chronicle* he wrote: "Mr. Beecher spoke for two hours in the midst of vociferous interruptions and stopped because of physical exhaustion. The only encouragement was a cheer for his courage when he retired. . . . In London Mr. Beecher conquered attention and did much to change public sentiment."[8]

Perhaps it was this admiration for Beecher and the institution of the church that would cause Thomson to commit another act of heroism shortly following the end of the Civil War. Thomson's daughter, Ethel, recollected her terror when St. George's Church, just around the corner from the Parton house, went up in flames. According to Ethel's recollection, her father dashed in to help bring out the historic Peter Stuyvesant chair.[9]

While Beecher grew in popularity following the Civil War, Thomson's work fell somewhat out of fashion. On September 9, 1865, an appraisal on American humor appeared in the *Brooklyn Daily Eagle* that wrote off Thomson as a has-been who, having locked on to one success with his first book, then began mass producing "hasty and ill-digested matter, which soon overshadowed and swallowed up the pleasant reputation he had so easily and deservedly won." The article went on to mention another humorist, Captain Derby, who seemed to have contained himself with a measured literary career and thereby sustained his success. So too had Thomson's friend and Pfaff's drinking pal Artemus Ward, according to the reviewer at the *Eagle*, who proclaimed that "the simple drollery of his writings is irresistible."[10]

In fact, after losing his job at the *Tribune*, Thomson was less prolific, and there seemed to be less demand for his Doesticks articles. The last book of substance Thomson wrote was *The Witches of New York*. At twenty pages in length, the Pierce Butler publication was more of a pamphlet.

Following the war, Thomson's brother Clifford returned to New York, taking up newspaper work at his brother's former paper, the *New-York Tribune*, then the *New York Times* and the *Evening Mail*. In 1877, he became editor-in-chief of the *Spectator*, a New York insurance newspaper. He would hold this position for thirty-four years. He was also a member of the Loyal Legion, the Medal of Honor Legion, the Life Insurance Underwriters Association, and the Automobile Club. He was noted as being the director of the Hudson Trust Company. While Clifford seems to have had the more responsible personality of the two brothers, he simultaneously continued to live in the shadow of his brother's fame. In 1865, the *Times Union* wrote, "Major Thomson, who is a brother of Mortimer Thomson, (Doesticks,) the well-known comic writer and lecturer, has served all through the war as an aid-de-camp on the staff of Major General Pleasonton."[11]

In May 1866, *Semi-Weekly Wisconsin* announced that Thomson had commenced a new series of humorous letters as Doesticks, which was being printed in *Street & Smith's New York Weekly*. The fiction magazine was started in 1855 by Francis Scott Street and Francis Shubael Smith and in the twentieth century became known for its pulp titles, both magazines and books. Thomson published articles with the magazine up to ten times a year, with his most prolific year being 1859. He continued writing the odd letter for them under the Doesticks pseudonym. The topics ranged from reflections on the madness of May Day (New Yorkers would move house on the same day every year), the absurdities of politics, the latest craze for velocipedes, the new fashion for eating horse meat, late-night cat wailing, the practice of calling on New Year's Day, and many others. To these articles, Thomson lent his mocking, absurd humor.

He also used this platform to ridicule women's suffrage and rights. He wrote, "Now I have a great respect for women as has any other person on the face of this created earth." Of course, the passage continues with a *but*: "I do really take leave to think that there is a fit and proper place for women just as I have no doubt there is for every thing on earth." He complained about the new postmistress, who was awarded the job in favor of apparently hundreds of male applicants. Thomson gave multiple examples of her incompetence in the first few days of her new job while she was in training (as if no man ever made a mistake at a new job). Thomson also surmised that women didn't understand or couldn't perform the demands of male work: "I imagine that women, when they aspire to the bank and the counting-room, think of nothing but the superficial features of the business, and never regard, because they can't see them, the heavy undertow of duties, cares and responsibilities that underlies the surface of business." If only men's work were as easy as a woman's, Thomson reasoned: "The ledger and cash book would be laid aside while the merchant would wield the broom and flourish the dust-rag with such a delightful sense of freedom from the cares of bonds, stocks, deeds, mortgages, bills payable and money affairs generally, as would make him as happy and light-hearted as a canary bird."[12]

A month earlier, on April 8, 1869, in the same periodical Thomson mocked the inevitability of a women's suffrage election day. Thomson claimed that once the Suffragettes had their way, the poor men would be doing housework—which, as we have seen, he would a month later argue would be a relaxing treat for the men. It would also just be a matter of time before women would be drinking the men's whiskey and smoking their cigars, upsetting the natural order of everything.

Perhaps in some way Thomson was nervous that women would surpass him in his own capabilities. In November 1867, the *Border Sentinel* reported that Thomson was studying medicine and had given up on reporting. However, later obituaries would state that he gave up on his medical degree and never became a doctor.

Around the same time, Thomson also began writing about his young son, Mark, under the pseudonym "Trumps." Mark was apparently learning German, and Thomson was engaging in his fatherly duties, attending Mark's performances at the German-American Institute. It is not clear whether Thomson was living with his son at the time, as he wrote about staying in a boarding house, yet in the 1870 census he was listed as living with his mother, Mark, and Clifford's family, which included Clifford's wife and two children.[13]

At the boarding house, he poked fun at the escapades of his landlady and fellow tenants on April Fools' Day: "They conspired with the cook to provide the most wonderful dishes for the table, so that when I undertook to eat a very nice looking 'doughnut' I only succeeded in getting my mouth full of *cotton*, which had been ingeniously disguised in batter and then fried in lard."[14]

Thomson made rare mention of his father in his writing, but on March 21, 1868, it was announced in the *New York Daily Herald* that Edwin Thomson had passed away at the age of sixty at the home of his sons on Forty-Third Street in south Brooklyn. According to his death certificate, he died of "debility," a term used for some undefined illness. A couple of short obituaries appeared in small, local newspapers (misspelling his last name "Thompson"), including the *Buffalo Morning Gazette* and *Yonkers Gazette*, which said he was "well-known and highly esteemed in Rochester, and subsequently in California and New York."[15] There were also some oddly brief and perhaps trite announcements that "Doesticks' [*sic*] father is dead"[16] in several newspapers, including the *Star Tribune*. While Edwin Thomson's name appears on the Green-Wood Cemetery "Thomson" tombstone purchased by Mortimer Thomson, there is little indication anywhere of the effect his father's death may have had on him or Clifford. Perhaps, though, it caused him to give up on his writing and look for a steadier source of income.

In 1869, a mysterious notice appeared in the *Leavenworth Times* stating that "Doesticks has a place in the office of one of the Collectors of Internal Revenue of New York city."[17] This note was later clarified in a letter that Thomson wrote to Samuel Clemens on October 21, 1870, in which he requested a copy of *The Innocents Abroad* be sent to him at the IRS office. With hilarious flare, Thomson scribed,

Come now, you inveterate old Galaxicuss trot out that book—place it, by proxy, (for I won't insist on your coming personally) where these far-reaching fingers can approach the said—then tell your prox to look the other way and the book will vanish. Or in-struct your agents here in York to send a copy, carriage paid and with the Government Stamp on, on a cart to yours truly at 45 Water St., where I at present suspend myself, being Storekeeper of a U. S. Bonded Warehouse, in the Internal Revenue Department of this model Government.[18]

A week later Clemens wrote to his publisher, Elisha Bliss, president of the American Publishing Company, requesting Thomson be sent a copy of the book. Thomson remained a storekeeper at the IRS for several years, as he was still listed as working there in the 1871–1872 *New York City Directory*, as well as living at 119 Dekalb Avenue in Brooklyn.

In the late 1860s, Rudd & Carleton, the book publisher of Josh Billings and Mortimer Thomson, had been eager to publish an almanac. The publisher had approached several of its humor writers, including Artemus Ward, Orpheus C. Kerr, Josh Billings, and Thomson, "but none of them took a fancy to the work."[19] In the end, Billings wrote a send-up of the *Farmers' Almanac* in 1870 with the popular slogan "Perhaps rain—perhaps not." It was so popular it sold ninety thousand copies, and Carleton paid Billings $35,000 as his share of the profits. Perhaps Thomson should have stooped to this variety of fortune telling to avoid the extreme debt in which he would later find himself.

On June 6, 1872, the *Star Tribune* in Minneapolis triumphantly declared, "It is with pleasure that we announce to the readers of the TRIBUNE that Mortimer Thomson, Esq., the veritable 'Doesticks,' so well and favorably known in the literary world, this morning assumes the chair of Associate Editor of this paper. Mr. Thomson is so well known to the reading public that it is unnecessary to commend him as a writer, of superior ability, rare humor, and keen wit."[20] In August of that year, the newspaper would also note that it was not only "ably supported" by Mortimer but also by his brother Clifford.

By all appearances, Thomson was welcomed as a star in Minnesota; in a way, it seemed he might get back on his literary feet in his new position. On September 14, 1872, the *Star Tribune* grandly announced that Thomson had followed the address of Hon. E. M. Wilson, the mayor of Minneapolis, with a "pithy and pointed poem."[21] The *Star Tribune*, however, did not print the poem, stating they did not have space.

In 1873, Thomson was said to have returned to New York City to take up a position as the editor at *Leslie's Illustrated Weekly*.[22] However, concerning notes on Thomson's decline continued to follow. On April 28 of the same year, the *Rutland Daily Herald* wrote a retrospective of American humor, stating:

> We can recall the wide popularity Doesticks (Mortimer Thomson) gained as a humorist. His Damphool was in everybody's mouth, and in many persons' character. His sketches were laughed at immoderately. He came over from Detroit, Mich., to New York and the *Tribune* and scintillated a year or two. Then he was pronounced wearisome, and ere long he sank out of sight.[23]

It is possible Thomson saw or heard about this article discussing his languishing literary career. The Rutland newspaper was based in Vermont, but given that Thomson was friends with a widely read literary set, he might have received word about this dismissive article.

It is hard to tell whether an article that appeared in the *Star Tribune* on May 1, 1873, was tongue-in-cheek or not, but it claimed that Thomson had grown "fat on bread and milk. His fighting weight is three hundred and fifty, and by August he expects to tip the scales at four hundred."[24] A later photograph of Thomson in Clifford's archives at the New-York Historical Society does show an older Thomson looking rather jowly. The next year, an unkind article regarding his looks also made its rounds in the press, which after stating how handsome and full of vivacity he had been twenty years before, "Now he is decidedly stout, not to say coarse, in appearance; his comeliness, all the fine line of his face, and his symmetry of figure have gone forever."[25] Journalists were uncharitably judging Thomson's middle-aged appearance, just as he had mocked the fortune tellers' looks in his youth.

From additional accounts, it becomes clear that Thomson was falling apart, both in health and finances. In the same year, James Parton wrote to Ellen Eldredge about bumping into Thomson on the street; he looked in terrible shape and had asked Parton for money. Replying to Ellen's concern, Parton had written a reassuring note:

> I have heard nothing additional from him—not even an acknowledgment of the money I have sent to him. Don't worry. He is utterly powerless—in body, in mind, in purse. He cannot maintain himself for a week—much less another. You need fear nothing. If he should apply to you for money, it would be madness in you to send it. Refer

the whole thing to me, and I will see if he cannot be got back to Minnesota, or into some institution.[26]

A letter from Thomson to Thurlow Weed, dated August 25, 1873, requested a loan of fifty dollars from Weed. Weed stated that Thomson had claimed to have been sick, that his nurse had pawned his clothing, and that he was in desperate need of money. Thomson said that he was asking Weed because he had already made "heavy drafts on my nearer friends."[27]

In June 1873, a stock market crash occurred in Europe, which in turn caused a panic in the United States, with investors selling off their investments, most particularly those in the railroads. This triggered a great depression, which lasted until 1878 and cast a gloomy pall over the nation. Perhaps this in turn ignited additional mental anguish in Thomson's own life, considering he was already in significant debt and poor health.

When Thomson's death, at the age of forty-two, was announced in 1875, several misleading articles about its cause appeared. Several obituaries stated he had died of heart disease. Other newspapers hinted that Thomson had dabbled in opium before he died. Thomson had at the very least experimented with opium, as confirmed in a humorous essay written in 1861, but there was no corroboration to be found that excessive use of opium had been the actual cause of death.

The official answer is in the archives of Green-Wood Cemetery, where Thomson had purchased his plot many years earlier, on April 30, 1860, just before he had gone to serve in the Civil War. He had noted his address as the *Tribune* office. The internment records state that Thomson died on June 25, 1875, from cirrhosis of the liver. It says he was a late resident of the Inebriate Asylum on Wards Island. In a sense, this is unsurprising given that newspapermen of the era were known to be heavy drinkers due to the long hours and pressure to constantly create content. Thomson was far from alone in his disease, as can also be observed from his visit to the Gipsy Girl. Moreover, William Sanger noted in his study of the prostitutes on Blackwell's Island that "in 1854, in the Penitentiary Hospital alone, more than fourteen hundred persons received medical assistance for delirium tremens and other maladies arising from excess in drinking."

In 1864 in New York City, the legislature passed an act authorizing the establishment of an inebriate asylum on Wards Island. Work began in 1866, and it was formally opened to the public on July 21, 1868. A three-story brick building, it cost $332,377.08 to build (just over $6 million in 2023 dollars). It was constructed to accommodate four hundred patients. Patients (or their families) paid to be committed to the Inebriate Asylum on a sliding scale. One class paid five dollars a week, another ten dollars, and a third would pay twelve or more dollars. The amount reflected the quality of accommodation offered. This was common practice in that era. For example, at the Smallpox Hospital on Blackwell's Island, the rich could be confined to a private room on the third floor, while the poor huddled together on the first and second floors.

According to a reporter in the *Corvallis Gazette-Times*, the new Inebriate Asylum was, sadly, a much-needed addition to New York City, and alcoholism was defined as a quintessentially *male* problem: "Thousands of men, not a few of whom belong to good society, are afflicted with delirium tremens. Drink overcomes the best of them. . . . In fact, drunkenness has become so general a disorder (it is proclaimed by the faculty to be a disease, now, you know) that a demand has arisen in every quarter for a hospital for its special treatment."[28]

An 1873 book by the Reverend John Francis Richmond, *New York and Its Institutions, 1609–1873*, detailed many of New York City's social institutions, many of which were built out of sight on the city's outer islands. According to Richmond, of the 339 patients admitted during the first six months of operation, only fifty-two paid for their time there. By 1871, 165 of the 1,270 patients admitted were paying guests. Records are not available that would confirm whether Thomson paid for his time there or not, but it is possible members of his family may have paid for his stay.

Richmond noted that the rules of the Inebriate Asylum on Wards Island were incredibly lax; patients were not restrained, paroles were easily granted, and every patient seemed intent on reform. However, Richmond observed, "This excessive kindness was subject to such continual abuse, that to save the Institution from utter demoralization a stricter discipline was very properly introduced."[29] Richmond did not detail what that discipline might have included. Richmond added that the asylum had an excellent library and a billiard room. Those were luxuries rarely seen in other institutions catering to the needy, such as almshouses for the poor, one of few options for the destitute before the Social Security Act of 1935.

Richmond sounded just like Thomson in his harsh judgment of the Gipsy Woman's alcoholism when he wrote: "Intemperance has been for ages the withering curse of the race in nearly every part of this world. It has feasted alike upon the innocency of childhood, the beauty of youth, the amiableness of woman, the talents of the great, and the experience of age."[30]

Although Richmond wrote a positive report on the Inebriate Asylum as an institution, cracks had begun to appear in 1872. The *Baltimore Sun* announced, "Grave charges of mismanagement have been brought against the officers of the Inebriate Asylum on Ward's [*sic*] Island. It is stated among other things that patients are frequently as drunk in the asylum as they possibly could be outside."[31] A year later, the *New York Times* released a more extensive report of "unpleasant rumors" concerning the management of the Inebriate Asylum, including favoritism toward those who paid, especially toward "wealthy men's sons"; claims that some men had been discharged for drinking rum or for owing one or two months' worth of board money; and accusations that few patients were cured. A *Times* reporter interviewed the manager, Dr. Fisher, who mostly defended his policies but did admit he thought the institution a failure because it was impossible to cure a man from drinking. The *Times* mentioned that Dr. Day of the Binghamton Asylum had claimed to have permanently cured 203 out of 228 patients; Dr. Fisher called that claim preposterous. Dr. Fisher went on to state that there were eighty to ninety patients in the asylum at that time, about twenty of whom were registered as first-class boarders. "All of them appear to be perfectly satisfied."[32] They all had access to the billiard room, reading room, and library. Even the second and third class of patients had good substantial food three times a day. Dr. Fisher mentioned there was a mix of clerks, bookkeepers, farmers, carpenters, merchants, druggists, physicians, housekeepers, teachers, reporters (like Thomson), musicians, authors, and lawyers. There were also twenty females housed in the east wing of the asylum.

It is hard to tell how much of Dr. Fisher's report was exaggerated. Such institutions were regularly called out for abuses perpetrated when the staff thought no one was looking. A year after this article and Richmond's report were released, another account in the *New York Times* on September 15, 1874, stated that the "Commissioners of Charities and Correction" were considering shutting it down. The *Times* said that the asylum had not paid its expenses in a "long time," even though its patients were charged for their keep. The *Times* concluded, "At present there are only ten inmates, and the amount received from them is much less than the expenses."[33]

Coincidentally, the Inebriate Asylum closed as an institution the same year that Thomson was housed there. The building was temporarily used for the overflow of patients from the Insane Asylum, also on Wards Island, and was briefly combined as the Inebriate Asylum and the Homeopathic Hospital. That Homeopathic Hospital became known as Wards Island Hospital. In 1894, that institution was moved to Blackwell's Island and renamed the Metropolitan Hospital. It was housed in the former Insane Asylum on Blackwell's Island, which had been exposed in 1887 by Nellie Bly in her series of articles for the *New York World*, published in book form as *Ten Days in a Mad-House*. This only serves to emphasize the malleability of these institutions.

Wards and Randall's Islands sit between the neighborhoods of Harlem in Manhattan and Astoria in Queens. Thomson would have been transported there by boat. Native Americans had called it Tenkenas, which has been variously translated as "Wild Lands" or "Uninhabited Place." In the mid-nineteenth century, Wards Island became home to several social institutions for the city, which Thomson may have witnessed during his time there. Those included a potter's field, which was relocated from the Madison Square and Bryant Park graveyards; the State Emigrant Refuge (a hospital for sick and destitute immigrants, where Emma Lazarus was inspired to write "The New Colossus," based on her time volunteering there); the New York City Insane Asylum; and, much later, a psychiatric center. Neighboring Randall's Island, which Wards Island would become connected to in the 1960s by landfill, also housed an orphanage, poor house, potter's field, "idiot" asylum, homeopathic hospital, reform school, and rest home for Civil War veterans.

Thomson died on June 25, 1875, at the Inebriate Asylum of cirrhosis of the liver in an age when little was known about this condition, let alone the treatment of alcoholism. Cirrhosis had only been given its name in an 1819 paper by Rene Laennec. The common cause of the disease is consumption of excessive alcohol. When a person drinks too much alcohol over the years, the liver becomes damaged and scarred. In the late stages of cirrhosis, the person's skin and eyes can become jaundiced, and there can be abdominal pain or swelling, loss of appetite, nausea and vomiting, itchy skin, weight loss, confusion, and disorientation. While Thomson did not leave any letters or diaries recording his decline in the Inebriate Asylum, given the effects of late-stage cirrhosis of the liver and the reputation of the institution where Thomson had passed, he likely did "not go gentle into that good night," and he would not live until the age of sixty-nine, as the Gipsy Girl predicted.

When Thomson visited the Gipsy Girl in 1857, he had more in common with her than just alcoholism and smallpox scars. The Gipsy Girl lived at No. 207 Third Avenue, between Eighteenth and Nineteenth Streets, just a few blocks from the well-to-do Stuyvesant Square and Gramercy Park where Thomson would live for a couple of years after his article came out.

Because of her generic name, it doesn't seem possible to find out the fate of the Gipsy Girl, but it is easy to imagine that she may have had a similar fate as Thomson, who mocked her fondness for gin. Since it was mostly taboo (except to some degree at Bohemian establishments and German saloons such as Pfaff's) for women to be out drinking in public, women's drinking would have been done in the home. While alcoholism in middle- and upper-class women (and men, for that matter) could be more easily hidden away in roomy apartments, for impoverished women living in crowded conditions, their alcoholism was on public display and could be discussed without discretion by such reporters as Thomson. While Thomson's demise and cause of death was publicly kept quiet, the Gipsy Girl's addiction was flaunted in the press and scorned by him.

Similarly, Thomson's smallpox was barely discussed in public. In his book and article, he ridiculed the Gipsy Girl's pockmarked face, only to catch the disease himself shortly after finishing his series of articles. Smallpox was highly contagious and spread through the air in droplets. It can also be spread through contaminated bedding or clothing. Hence the high risk for those like the Gipsy Girl, who lived in crowded tenements.

The Gipsy Girl is hard to trace partly because she had the kind of name commonly used by other fortune tellers. For example, other fortune tellers called themselves the Gipsy Palmist, Gipsy Woman, or Gipsy Wonder. Later, their names would become Madame York or Madame Duval.

What is also fascinating is her decision to use the name "The Gipsy Girl." The word "gipsy" was originally used to describe a nomadic people, the Romani, who came from northern India. They started entering Europe around the ninth and tenth centuries and were called gypsies because Europeans incorrectly assumed they were from Egypt. Today, the term is considered an ethnic slur by the Romani people, who for centuries were persecuted throughout Europe. They mostly worked in low-level jobs that could be performed wherever they traveled, including as tinsmiths, cobblers, tool makers, musicians, dancers, circus animal trainers, and of course, fortune tellers. Although the Romani were mostly treated with scorn by Europeans, they also attracted a certain amount of intrigue for their exoticness. While it is not clear from the text whether the Gipsy Girl was descended from the Romani people, it is likely this romantic European curiosity about the other that the Gipsy Girl was hoping to attract.

Like Mrs. Hayes, the Gipsy Girl was also the subject of an article in the

New York Times in 1855, when she was living at 5 Wooster Street. At that time, the advertised Gipsy Girl promised to be so "skilled in palmistry and could impart a secret (charge extra) by which one might be enabled to win the affections of the opposite sex." The reporter proceeded to the abode of the Gipsy Girl with his friend "Damon" at seven o'clock in the evening. He reported that the door was opened by a "tawny-looking girl, with restless eyes and a black velvet basque." It seems likely this reporter influenced Thomson, as his imagination also conjures up absurdly overwrought imaginings of gypsies with "toads tamed and intelligent. Smoke-dried old women, heirs to all the wisdom of Solomon, and talking Rommany. Black hens, and sable cats—in short, all the paraphernalia of witchcraft."[34] To the reporter's disappointment, however, all he found, of course, was a woman down on her luck and doing her best to make a living in a time and place of limited options.

The reporter professed himself to be nervous at being shut up alone with this "wild-looking" woman, who, to his surprise, "conducted herself peaceably." Like any other palm reader, she requested his palm and palpated it, examining its lines, muscles, and flesh. The Gipsy Girl gave a reading full of the usual vague pronouncements: The reporter would have "ups and downs." While he was not wealthy, he was not poor either. He had losses but was born under a fortunate star. The reporter described the reading as being delivered in "one breathless monotonous stream." He said the palmist could not tell him a single concrete detail, such as his profession, country, or when and where he was born. The reporter then made some racist observations, writing that "the house reeked of Spaniards. Twice did swarthy sons of Hispaniola thrust their garlicky heads into the room while my fortune was being told." The reporter paid his fee and exited the room to find "poor Damon glaring at an unwashed Spaniard."[35] Again, his pity was directed toward his "poor," presumably middle-class friend, who had been thrust among the "riffraff."

The Gipsy Girl cannot be traced in the *New York City Directory* or through the Third Avenue address cited by Thomson. However, some fascinating news items appeared in connection with the addresses where she had potentially lived. For example, on March 30, 1871, investigators at the Eighth Precinct discovered on the roof of 5 Wooster Street a skull "of a grown person who had been dead a great many years."[36] Such a report would likely have excited the imaginations of Thomson and the former unidentified ink slinger of the 1855 article.

While ultimately no connection between Thomson's Gipsy Girl and the Gipsy Palmist at 419 Canal Street have been established, a telling report was published in the *New York Daily Herald* on Valentine's Day, 1874. The article discussed a hearing on relief for the destitute at St. John's Chapel on Varick Street, between Laight and Beach. The *Herald* had run an appeal for the poor, and three thousand dollars had been raised. The *Herald* then conducted a hearing to decide who was the most deserving of aid. Among those heard was a Mrs. S of 419 Canal Street, "a delicate looking woman." She had three children of ages five years, two years, and seven months. Her husband had been unemployed for over three months in an era when there was no social security and men were the expected breadwinners. According to the *Herald*, "They have now been clothed and fed, and their wants will be attended to."[37] One can imagine the Gipsy Palmist could have had similar struggles as Mrs. S. These newspaper appeals did not often occur, and chance of success in winning relief was slim. Moreover, the article does not mention how much aid this family was provided or how long that aid was to last.

Could the Gipsy Girl have had a similar fate to Thomson's, spending her last days at the Inebriate Asylum on Wards Island? It seems possible. After all, the Inebriate Asylum welcomed the poor, middle, and upper classes alike, as well as women. Is it possible that during his final breaths, Thomson recognized just how much he had in common with the women he had mocked?

Chapter 8

Mrs. Seymour

Lenormand Card: Coffin (Meaning = *Loss, Grief, Mourning*)

Mrs. Seymour's advertisement claimed, just as Mrs. Hayes's had, that she was "the most successful medical and business Clairvoyant in America."[1] Doesticks believed that spiritualists were the snobs of the witch world because they considered Bibles, keys, magic mirrors, and cards beneath their dignity. He opened his article on Mrs. Seymour by noting some of the more famous spiritualists, such as Cora Hatch and her table-tipping trick and the rappings of the Fox sisters.

Mrs. Seymour's abode at 110 Spring Street was "not more seedy in appearance than the majority of half-way decent tenant houses, which all have a decrepit look after they are four or five years old, as though youthful dissipations had made them weak in the joints. . . . It is a house where a man on a small salary would apply for cheap board." Doesticks knocked at the door of the tenant house and was greeted by a "frowzy, coarse, plump, semi-respectable girl."[2] He thought she needed a wash. The young lady escorted Doesticks into the reception room, where he was afforded time to make his snooty judgments about the lair into which he had entered. There was little furniture, but at least it was neat, he thought. From an apartment with folding doors, he could hear the scraping of a saucepan. The young lady disappeared into this spot, and moments later Mrs. Seymour appeared.

Doesticks judged her to be about thirty-five years old. She had dark hair and eyes, protruding lips and a heavy chin, and was of medium height. She was a slow-moving and self-possessed woman, which Doesticks found

112

"repelling and chilly." Mrs. Seymour looked at Doesticks, rightly it would seem, with suspicion. She glanced around to see if all the objects of the room were still in order. Her demeanor was so frosty toward Doesticks that "he would as soon have wedded an iceberg."[3] Doesticks told her about his purpose in venturing to Spring Street. He wanted to know about the present well-being of his "absent friends." At this, Mrs. Seymour walked to the door, apparently without taking her eyes from his hands and pockets, summoning him into another room.

There, Mrs. Seymour sat down in a rocking chair and closed her eyes. The young lady who answered the door walked into the room and stood behind Mrs. Seymour's chair. She pressed her thumbs firmly into Mrs. Seymour's temples for two minutes, and then the spiritualist seemed to fall into a trance and freeze up. The young lady made some mesmeric gestures over Mrs. Seymour, who appeared to be sleeping. To Doesticks's horror, the young lady then placed the very cold hand of Mrs. Seymour's into his hand. "The worst of it was that Mrs. Seymour's hand is not an agreeable one to hold; it is cold and flabby, and not suggestive of vitality,"[4] he wrote.

Her face froze, her lips thin and blue. Doesticks, who had clearly not been to a séance before, did not know what to do. The awkwardness was broken by the corpse-like Mrs. Seymour asking him, "Where am I to go?" Doesticks instructed her to go to Minnesota. At that prompt, Mrs. Seymour told Doesticks she saw two *very* old people, one a man and the other a woman. One of them had been very sick with a bilious fever but was feeling better. The pair may be husband and wife. Mrs. Seymour also saw a young male and female pair. She could not envision much of the young man, but the young lady was tall with dark, straight hair. She was pretty and agreeable and had apparently had a very severe attack of illness from which she had recently recovered. She was not a healthy woman, however. She would not live a long life and would die in six to eight years. Mrs. Seymour could not tell the circumstances under which she would die.

All four people were anxious about Doesticks because they had not heard from him recently. They had written to him twice within the last three months but for one reason or another had not heard back. The foursome was apparently not happy with Minnesota but would hang around for the spring when Doesticks would be visiting. Mrs. Seymour instructed Doesticks to visit the post office, as one of their letters was sitting there right now.

Doesticks observed that Mrs. Seymour was delivering her predictions in a jerky and twitching manner, violently clasping his hand. He wrote that he had friends in Minnesota, but none of the particulars Mrs. Seymour related seemed to match the description of any of his friends. Giving Mrs. Seymour the benefit of the doubt, he pressed her for further details, but she seemed to dodge Doesticks's questions with more generalities. He became increasingly frustrated with her evasions and inability to describe accurately any of his Minnesota friends. He was impatient for the séance to come to an end.

However, Doesticks did not know what to do to wake this frosty lady. There was an awkward pause, and he considered calling for Mrs. Seymour's maid. Just in time, however, Mrs. Seymour opened her eyes and called for her assistant, who came back into the room and made a few more gestures toward Mrs. Seymour, as if to wake her from her trance. Doesticks paid the newly alert Mrs. Seymour a dollar and left.

In June 1875, it was Thomson who was mourned as an "absent friend." Following his death at the inebriate asylum, he was buried by James Winterbottom & Co., an undertaking business founded in 1849. *New York's Great Industries* described it as "well-known and highly reputable."[5] The information about who paid for Thomson's funeral does not seem to be available, though it is highly likely it was his brother Clifford, since he signed the legal document stating Thomson had not left a will but had two children. The descriptions of the funeral service and burial at Green-Wood Cemetery, however, make it clear that Thomson continued to be loved and remembered fondly among his artist friends. It is not mentioned if either of his children attended the funeral, but it was unlikely they were there, because Ethel was then settled in Newburyport, Massachusetts, and Mark was living in Minnesota with the Van Cleve family. It would have taken days for either one of them to reach New York City.

It is likely his brother Clifford and mother, Sophia, who were still in New York at the time, would have attended the funeral. While we can only imagine the grief Sophia must have felt at her son's passing, a poem she wrote for the *Michigan Argus* under the pseudonym Rosamund, which was published on March 19, 1851, offers a window of insight:

> The spell is broke—the household chain is riven,
> And one bright link is severed from the rest;
> Yet who would slay that rapturous song of heaven,
> That lingers on his harp-strings 'mong the blest?

They've laid that lov'd form in the lonely grave—
The heavy sods are pressing on his breast—
They've sung his requiem—like the moaning wave
It floated o'er the sleeper in his rest.

And the bereaved household—can no light
Through their dark spirits send a cheering ray?
Their idol's shattered—withering and blight
Have fallen upon him—he has passed away.

They'll miss him. Aye, at mourn, and noon, and eve,
And think they hear his footstep on the stair;
Then crush their tears, and turn away and grieve,
For 'tis another's step—he is not there.

His mother—but no words of mine can tell
The deep, deep anguish of that stricken heart:
The iron entered when the mandate fell
That crush'd her flower and saw her hopes depart.

A detailed report of the funeral service appeared in the *New-York Herald*. It took place on a blazing hot Sunday at one o'clock in the afternoon,

> when a hearse rumbled over the stones in Twenty-ninth street and halted at the gate of the 'Little Church Around the Corner.' Six or eight coaches were already waiting along the curb, the drivers standing listlessly about in the shade of the trees. A group of gentlemen who had come singly, in pairs and in clusters, and who were inside the railing, took off their hats as the undertaker and his assistant carried a rosewood casket, blazing with silver ornamentation under the hot rays of the sun, into the church.

The *Herald* article continued: "Previously there had gone by some flowers, and their delicious aroma lingered ghost-like on the breeze."[6] The report mentioned brilliant floral displays, sent mostly by staff members of the Frank Leslie office, including a broken column, a wreath, a star, a heart, and an anchor—coincidentally all symbols that appear in the Lenormand deck. Captain James B. Mix of the post office had sent an envelope of flowers, with a postage stamp of buds, bearing the inscription, "M. Thomson, New York Press." Another article in the *Buffalo Morning Express* complained that the flowers were too ostentatious and marked the development of a garish trend. "This 'mammoth envelope,'" the article sneered, "so ingeniously constructed, was not only a vulgar bit of 'shop,' but it was as essentially offensive at such a solemn time as it would have been for the clergyman to indulge in puns in his prayer or to quote jokes from Doesticks' 'Elephant Club' during his 'brief remarks.'"[7]

Few would disagree with the appropriateness of where Thomson's funeral service was conducted. The official name of the "Little Church around the Corner" is the Church of the Transfiguration. It was founded in 1848 by the Rev. Dr. George Hendric Houghton, and the building dates from 1850. Rev. Dr. Houghton's vision for the church was that it should serve as a refuge for the poor and marginalized. The reverend welcomed all regardless of race, class, or background. It was a stop on the Underground Railroad, sheltering escaped slaves making their way north. It was also a refuge for African Americans during the 1863 New York City Draft Riots.

Just a few days before Christmas, 1870, Joseph Jefferson, an actor who had become famous for his portrayal of Rip Van Winkle, had approached the rector of the Church of the Atonement. He requested a funeral for his friend and fellow actor George Holland. Acting was considered low-level, disreputable work in 1870, undertaken by drunks, prostitutes, gamblers, and destitute types, such as fortune tellers, perhaps. The rector refused to conduct a service for this riffraff. Jefferson was persistent, and eventually the rector admitted there was a "little church around the corner" that might be able to help him. Jefferson replied, "Then I say to you, sir, God bless the little church around the corner."[8] The church has since maintained ties with the theater, serving as the national headquarters of the Episcopal Actors' Guild since its founding in 1923.

Perhaps the Church of the Atonement was cursed for its actions: It is no longer there, but the Little Church around the Corner still exists and was made a national landmark in 1973. The church has been called a tranquil haven by New Yorkers looking for peace in their hectic city. Just off from chaotic Fifth Avenue, there is a delightful garden at the front with a lychgate, benches, and sculptures for contemplation, all of which were added after Thomson's time.

The press noted that the service was conducted by the founder of the church, Rev. Dr. Houghton, and that some of the pallbearers were Algernon S. Sullivan (a New York City lawyer), Commissioner W. H. Stiner (the excise commissioner who had been written about in Frank Leslie's paper), Henry Leslie (the eldest son of Frank Leslie and a member of the Scribbler's Club), and Caleb Dunn (a journalist who had worked at the *Tribune*, member of the Scribbler's Club, and patron of Pfaff's). The coffin was covered with floral tributes from the post office, Frank Leslie's establishment, the Scribbler's Club (a Bohemian association with offices on Thirteenth Street and composed of literary men, actors, and kindred spirits), and other friends.

The mourners at the Little Church around the Corner took a ferry from South Street to Green-Wood Cemetery in Brooklyn (the Brooklyn Bridge had not yet been built). Green-Wood Cemetery was established in 1838 and was influenced by Mount Auburn's opening in Cambridge, Massachusetts. Designed by David Bates Douglass, it was the original idea of the Brooklyn businessman Henry Evelyn Pierrepont. Initially, no one paid much attention to the new cemetery until DeWitt Clinton, the New York governor who had presided over the construction of the Erie Canal, was disinterred from Albany and moved to Green-Wood, where a monument was erected to him. Suddenly, all fashionable and wealthy New Yorkers wanted to be buried there. By the early 1860s, it was the greatest tourist attraction in the United States outside of Niagara Falls. Known for its rolling hills, sweeping views of the city, manmade ponds, and luscious and varied trees, Victorians would come to Green-Wood Cemetery for picnics in the days before Central Park was created. By the time Thomson was buried there, some of its other notables included Samuel Morse, Horace Greeley (the founder of the *New-York Tribune*), James Gordon Bennett Sr. (the founder of the *New-York Herald*), Henry Jarvis Raymond (the founder of the *New York Times*), Jeremiah Hamilton (the only Black millionaire in New York at the time of the Civil War), Elias Howe (the inventor of the sewing machine), Laura Keene (the actress who was on stage when Lincoln was shot), Hezekiah Pierrepont (the founder of Brooklyn Heights and father of Henry Evelyn Pierrepont), William "Bill the Butcher" Poole (a member of the Bowery Boys gang), and other prominent New Yorkers. When Henry Ward Beecher died in 1887, he was also buried at Green-Wood Cemetery.

Thomson's granite tombstone is a quick one-minute trip halfway up the hill from that of Charlotte Canda, who is known for accidentally designing her own mausoleum when she was only sixteen years old. She was killed on her seventeenth birthday when she was returning home for her party in a storm. Thrown from the carriage when the horses bolted, spooked by something, she died in the arms of her parents. Originally, Charlotte had designed the monument for her recently deceased aunt, and her father had adapted the design to include symbols of things Charlotte had loved, including musical and drawing instruments, sculptures of her pet parrots, and books. The Gothic Revival monument cost more than $45,000 to build at that time (approximately $1.5 million today) and became a major attraction when it was added to the cemetery in 1848. Up the hill from the monument, Thomson's slab is far more modest.

At Green-Wood Cemetery, an elegy was read by Mr. Franklin J. Ottarson, a successful New York journalist, editor (formerly at the *New York-Tribune* and later at the *New York Times*), and civil servant, who was also noted for drinking at Pfaff's.

Thomson's headstone was not lonely. It included the names of his first and second wives; his father, Edwin; and his mother, Sophia, who would be buried there eight years later.

While Thomson had become less prominent over the years as a writer and was mostly disparaged by humor critics in the press, in death there were many who still remembered him fondly. Multiple obituaries appeared in the *Star Tribune, Baltimore Sun, Brooklyn Union, Galveston Daily News, Kansas Chief, Owensboro Examiner, Philadelphia Inquirer, New York Times, Worthington Advance*, and other notable publications. Given the floral arrangements and attendants at his funeral, he was clearly still respected among his fellow journalists.

At the same time Thomson's death was being announced in the newspapers, Henry Ward Beecher's trial and scandal, in which he was accused of committing adultery with Elizabeth Tilton, a married woman, were making front-page news. Beecher's name was cleared at trial. However, he was pressured to retire from his position at Plymouth Church, and he spent the rest of his working days touring the country, giving lectures. His polemics continued to attract vast crowds, some drawn by curiosity to see the fallen preacher. Beecher was allowed to continue practicing and making an income. His original accuser, Victoria Woodhull, also a spiritualist, did her best to keep out of the public eye for the rest of her days, marrying a wealthy English banker.

Following Thomson's death, his name would appear in the press now and then. In February 1883, a few notices appeared stating that Mrs. Sophia Edna Thomson had passed away in Orange, New Jersey. She was noted as being the mother of Mortimer Thomson and Clifford Thomson, a New York editor. Two years later, Mrs. C. O. Van Cleve (Anna's mother) was reported by the *Star Tribune* to have received a telegram announcing the death of her grandson, Mark Thomson, at Deadwood, Montana. It was also stated that Mark was the son of Mortimer Thomson. In 1890, when Charles Pfaff died, as the proprietor of Pfaff's, he was said to have been associated with notable artists including Mortimer Thomson. In 1891, obituaries appeared for James Parton, one of which mentioned he had raised Ethel Parton, "the child of Mrs. Mortimer Thomson (the wife of 'Doesticks')."[9] Finally, in 1911, at the passing of Sol Eytinge, it was remembered that Mortimer Thomson had been present at his wedding.

Perhaps one of the most significant posthumous appearances of the work of Q. K. Philander Doesticks, P.B., was an article by him that was included in an anthology titled *Mark Twain's Library of Humor* and published in 1888. Samuel Clemens had chosen Doesticks's essay "A New Patent Medicine Operation."

In 1890, Thomson's first Niagara Falls article as Doesticks was also included in a 570-page, lavishly illustrated anthology, *Kings of the Platform and Pulpit*, by Melville D. Landon (Eli Perkins), published by Belford-Clarke Co. (later published by the Werner Company). The anthology contained works by such luminaries of the age as Artemus Ward, Mark Twain, Horace Greeley, and Henry Ward Beecher, among others. Unfortunately, Thomson's bio entry is riddled with factual errors, including spelling Thomson with a *p*, writing his pseudonym as "K. Q. Philander Doesticks," writing his middle initial as *M*, and stating that he was the brother of Fanny Fern.

Occasional articles would appear from time to time with a combination of serious and amusing anecdotes. For example, the time that J. Sterling Morton did not deny he was "Doesticks," or when Thomson heard a "howling mob" of four thousand listen to Henry Ward Beecher as he spoke in St. George's Hall, Liverpool.[10] It was remembered that Thomson had once posed as an army chaplain during the Civil War and that he had partied with the Prince of Wales (later King Edward VII), to the chagrin of the Duke of Newcastle.

Another article in the *Middletown Times* on January 30, 1917, discussed the debate concerning who had authored *Wa-wa-wanda: A Legend of Old Orange*. There had been speculation Thomson was the author of that text, which is set in Orange County. As the son-in-law of Fanny Fern, he was related to Nathaniel P. Willis, who lived in Orange County, and therefore must have visited it on occasion. However, as the author of the article noted, Fanny Fern was not close to her brother. Also, Q. K. Philander Doesticks, P.B., was not the kind of man to write a book that did not have his name on it.

Buried six feet under in Green-Wood Cemetery, survived by only two children who had little remembrance of him, and mostly panned in the press as a lesser humorist than Mark Twain and Artemus Ward, there were few still living who would be inclined to enlist a spiritualist's services to try to contact him as an "absent friend."

▟▟▟

The death of middle-aged men was not uncommon in the nineteenth century. Mrs. Seymour, famed for contacting the dead, first appeared in the press in December 1853, in an article titled "The Clairvoyant Case—Sudden Death of Mr. Stuyvesant."[11] Mr. John R. Stuyvesant was descended from Peter Stuyvesant, the grouchy, tyrannical, militant, peg-legged Dutch governor general. Peter Stuyvesant had spent his retirement on his plot of land, called the "Bouwerji," a seventeenth-century Dutch word for "farm." That farm was in today's East Village, which as the city grew north, became more and more valuable property for descendants of Peter Stuyvesant. Among the more notable of them is Petrus Peter Stuyvesant (1727–1805), a landowner, merchant, and philanthropist. This is the same Peter Stuyvesant whose chair Thomson was alleged to have rescued from a fire at St. George's Episcopal Church in Stuyvesant Square.

In this court case, Dr. John K. Seymour (the husband of Mrs. Seymour) was arrested on Stuyvesant's complaint that Seymour, "a man of genteel appearance,"[12] was fraudulently obtaining from him a deed of house and lot on Sixteenth Street, with an estimated value upward of eight thousand dollars. He was middle aged and had a wife and two children, all living in Poughkeepsie. He had previously tried to get his money back from the Superior Court but failed. His appeal to Justice Osbourne, in conjunction with District Attorney Blunt for criminal redress, however, had succeeded in going to trial.

Stuyvesant claimed that earlier that year he'd had a severe pain in his breast and had gone to visit Mrs. Seymour, the clairvoyant who promised to cure all diseases. At the time of this incident, the Seymours were located on Division Street, though during their trial they were living at 491 Houston Street. One of Mrs. Seymour's earliest advertisements from January 1852 said that she was working with *Miss* Seymour at Division Street, and, as well as professing to cure all diseases, she also said she could reveal the "whereabouts of absent friends."[13]

Mrs. Seymour allegedly sold her services for one dollar, and Dr. Seymour had also sold the "medicine" she prescribed at one to three dollars a bottle. Stuyvesant claimed that during these visits, "Mrs. Seymour, by her responses and acts, while in a clairvoyant state, invited liberties to be taken with her person by him, gradually and artfully leading him on, thereby placing him in a position which he now believes was done to carry out the design for the purpose of extorting money and property from him."[14] One night in May, she told Stuyvesant her husband was out of town in Boston and gave Stuyvesant a night latch key to the front door, inviting him to visit her the next night when the servants would be out of the way. Stuyvesant did as he was instructed the next night, and he deduced from her "seductive advances and artifices" that she had invited him to visit her bedroom. Just when Stuyvesant and Mrs. Seymour were in a state of partial undress, she suddenly slammed the door three times, which Stuyvesant later believed to be a signal to her husband, who immediately rushed into the room with a drawn sword cane, hitting Stuyvesant over the head with it several times. He accused Stuyvesant of seducing his wife and threatened to take his life unless he paid him a certain sum of money or its equivalent. Mr. Seymour had possession of Stuyvesant's clothing and refused to allow him to dress until he paid the money. At this, Stuyvesant, who claimed to be very frightened, agreed to transfer a deed of his house and lot on Sixteenth Street. Further, Stuyvesant claimed that Mrs. Seymour was a phony clairvoyant who made false claims about her powers.

The court was to hear testimony from the Seymours the following Thursday, but at the appointed hour, alarming news was received that Stuyvesant had died that morning, of Asiatic cholera, at the house of a relative on Second Avenue near Ninth Street. Rumors were circulated that the death was a suicide, but no one was allowed to make any assumptions until the coroner had conducted a postmortem examination. The last report about his death appeared in the *Brooklyn Daily Eagle* on December 9 and stated Stuyvesant was poisoned, but there was uncertainty as to how the poison was administered.

The magistrate, Justice Osborne, decided to issue a warrant for the arrest of Mr. Seymour, who appeared before court again on the Saturday evening, at which time he defended himself by stating that no felony existed in the matter and that he had a perfect right to compromise any attempted assault on his wife. Several days later, Mr. Seymour's counsel procured a writ of habeas corpus and brought the case before Judge Mitchell, who, on hearing the facts, remanded the matter back to the police magistrate, Justice Osborne. When the evidence showing the death of Mr. Stuyvesant was produced, Osbourne dismissed the charge and left Mr. Seymour free to go.

Because there were so few eyewitnesses to this bizarre event, and as Mrs. Seymour's account was missing from the story, it is difficult to know what to make of it. How might this situation have played itself out had Stuyvesant not died at the last moment? Had Mrs. Seymour indeed lured Stuyvesant over for a nighttime rendezvous with the hopes of trapping him through extortion? Or had Stuyvesant, an entitled wealthy man, a

Harvey Weinstein of his day, obtained a key through nefarious means and genuinely upset the family to such a degree that they demanded financial compensation?

This was not to be Mrs. Seymour's last run-in with the law. When Doesticks's 1857 articles began appearing in the *Tribune*, they were often printed alongside scandalous details of the gruesome murder of Harvey Burdell and the subsequent trial of Emma Cunningham. Thomson was aware of this and pointed out Mrs. Seymour's famed role as a peculiar witness at the trial in his articles. Doesticks devoted an entire paragraph to this matter, knowing his audience would be thoroughly aware of the particulars of the case, as it was being followed with lurid enthusiasm. George Templeton Strong would note in his diary on a Wednesday night, February 4, 1857: "Through all this miserable weather a crowd of several hundred people of all classes is in permanent position in front of the house. Well dressed women occupy the doorsteps of houses on the opposite side of Bond Street, stare steadily at #31, and seemed to derive relief from protracted contemplation of its front door."[15]

Harvey Burdell, a dentist living on opulent Bond Street, had been found murdered in his own house. His servants discovered him covered in blood, strangled, with fifteen stab wounds. His violent death sent shock waves through New York society. The scandal erupted further when Emma Cunningham, his lover, was arrested. The warring couple had been known for their tempestuous arguments. Cunningham was of the lower class and wanted to make herself an honest woman by marrying Burdell, and he had continuously refused her, carrying on other affairs and refusing to legitimize the match through marriage.

Victorian sensibility was horrified and beguiled by the idea of a murderess, and newspapers were saturated with accounts of this female monster. Eventually, Cunningham was acquitted, and the murder was never solved. Some present-day conjecture offers compelling theories that strongly suggest Cunningham was likely indeed innocent.

Newspaper accounts at the time paid an enormous amount of attention to the trial, and one witness who stood out was none other than Elizabeth Jane Seymour. On February 4, 1857, Mrs. Seymour arrived at court to provide testimony regarding the Burdell and Cunningham affair. Emma Cunningham had apparently consulted with Mrs. Seymour several times. According to Mrs. Seymour, at first Cunningham wanted to know about money some man owed her and about her daughter, who was sick. Cunningham was afraid her daughter's lungs were diseased. Later, Mrs. Seymour had found some business cards in her husband's pockets for houses of ill repute. The Seymours did live at 110 Spring Street, a five-minute walk from Burdell's posh street address, though in the seedier part of SoHo, which, according to *The Gentleman's Directory*, was at the time the heart of Manhattan's red-light district. Mrs. Seymour ventured that the business cards had been given to her husband by Emma Cunningham, who apparently requested that Mr. Seymour investigate Dr. Burdell's whereabouts and whether he was pursuing any illicit affairs. Dr. Burdell was said to have also visited Mrs. Seymour to discover why Cunningham was meeting with the clairvoyant.

Mrs. Seymour's testimony was at times irritatingly vague and full of contradictions about her life, perhaps because she was trying to hide some of its illicit history from the court. She had been married for ten or eleven years, she thought, but later she changed that to eight years, the length of time she had been in Manhattan. She was twenty-seven or twenty-eight years old, she said, but didn't even know her precise age. She had gone by the names Allen (her maiden name), Seymour, and Kelley. She was born in Augusta, Maine, and said she had lived in Boston almost all her life, but also Manhattan for eight years. At one point in the testimony, she claimed to know her husband a week before she married him; at another, she claimed to have known him a year before they wed. She couldn't quite remember where she had been married but vaguely recollected a location near Grand and Broome. She didn't know what her husband did for a living, but when she first met him, he was in the "grocery business in a small way."[16] He was now sick with rheumatism.

That same day, the *New York Herald* obtained an interview with Mrs. Seymour, who was being imprisoned for having talked to Emma Cunningham before the trial. The reporter called her a "gaily dressed lady . . . about thirty years of age, five feet high, light brown eyes, very dark hair, and not a very light complexion. She was dressed in a fine blue silk dress, cashmere shawl, with a gold brooch fastening, new kid gloves, and a rather showy hat."[17] The description of Mrs. Seymour as a young woman in fancy dress was surprising, given Thomson's depiction of her as a withered hag with cold, clammy hands.

Mrs. Seymour told the reporter that she had not been arrested but merely subpoenaed and that she was in jail for false reasons. She had never talked to Emma Cunningham but had been moved to the same room in which Cunningham was stationed because she had requested to be near a fire. She complained to the reporter that her business had suffered following this incident.

Two weeks later, she filed a suit against Coroner Connery for false imprisonment, for a steep ten thousand dollars in damages. According to her earlier interview with the *New York Herald*, she had been falsely arrested for discussing trial matters with Emma Cunningham. Mrs. Seymour claimed she had merely seen Cunningham in passing and had been wrongly imprisoned in a "comfortless cell" with nothing but a plank to rest on. She had also been annoyed and insulted by a crowd of people who presumed she had something to do with the murder when, according to Mrs. Seymour, she only knew Cunningham because she had consulted her as a clairvoyant. The suit was forgotten in the press, but it seems likely it was dismissed, as Mrs. Seymour continued to practice fortune telling in similarly dilapidated living quarters after 1857.

Perhaps because she had become so adept at dealing with officers of the law, in the series of arrests of fortune tellers that took place in 1858, Mrs. Seymour was not among those charged and held in custody, because "the lady did not profess to tell fortunes, but used her professed powers in cases of sickness and disease."[18] In the eyes of the law, it seems fortune telling was only considered illegal and harmful if the clairvoyant was guessing at lottery numbers or dating instead of addressing serious issues of disease, illness, and death. Perhaps the authorities felt that if they prosecuted the fortune tellers for medical advice they would be inching too close to arresting quack doctors, an occupation ruled by men. Or perhaps because Mrs. Seymour had been in trouble with the law several times previously, she knew better how to make it work to her advantage. It does seem odd that Mrs. Seymour was not arrested, even though her practice was very close to that of Mrs. Hayes and others who were arrested; perhaps she bribed the officers.

According to city records and newspapers, Mrs. Seymour moved farther and farther uptown. She was last heard from in 1871, promising "diseases discovered and cured."[19] But death is a guarantee for us all, and we must succumb to some disease or ailment eventually. Mrs. Seymour was last listed in the *New York City Directory* in 1871–1872 as living at 23 Horatio Street as the widow of John.

Concluding Remarks

At the end of *The Witches of New York*, Doesticks offered this merry conclusion:

> A recapitulation of the various prophecies made to the Cash Customer would show that he has been promised thirty-three wives, and something over ninety children—that he was brought into the world on various occasions between 1820 and 1833—that he was born under nearly all the planets known to astronomers—that he has more birth-places than he has fingers and toes—that he has passed through so many scenes of unexpected happiness and complicated misfortune in his past life, that he must have lived fifty hours to the day and been wide awake all the time—and he has so many future fortunes marked out for him that at three hundred and fifty years old his work will not be half done, and when at last all is finally accomplished, a minute dissection of his aged corpus will be necessary, that his earthly remains may be buried in all the places set down for him by these prophets.[1]

While this denouement is amusing, when customers on tours and talks ask me whether any of the fortune tellers were "any good," I find myself struggling to come up with a straightforward answer. According to Doesticks's accounts, they were all universally lousy. But of course, "good" is a highly subjective evaluation and dependent on the expectations of the person receiving the reading. As far as Doesticks was concerned, the fortune tellers did not make good on their promises to predict future relationships, iden-tify the name of the person they were reading, connect him with absent friends, and so forth. However, Doesticks did not visit them with an open mind. We also only have the accounts of Doesticks and the reporter at the *New York Times*, both of whom worked for newspapers invested in expos-ing the corrupt practices of fortune tellers. We do not have accounts from anyone who visited the fortune tellers in good faith or who may have gone for any of the reasons noted in the introduction, such as entertainment, therapy, companionship, practical advice, and so forth.

Occasionally, I have received comments from people who want to de-fend the abilities of the fortune tellers. "But many of them did predict he would marry twice," they say. That may be the case, but they also predicted a lot of other things that were dead wrong. Plus, predicting that a man in the mid-nineteenth century would be married twice is a safe guess. It is also the kind of prediction that would be hard to prove wrong until one is at the very end of one's life, unless he were to be married more than twice by the end of it.

In Susan Fair's book, she joked that Madame Prewster predicted the name of Doesticks's true love on her second guess as "Anna." However, she did also guess Emma, Ella, Jane, Etta, Lucy, and Cora before settling decisively on the name Mary.

Even if Doesticks's portrayal of the fortune tellers as outrageously bad and corrupt clairvoyants is accurate, they were sensational as busi-nesspeople. These women had tapped into one of the few corners of the nineteenth-century capitalistic markets that they, as people on the margins of society, could fill. They knew how to market themselves. The promises made in their advertisements were compelling. They were also savvy in their use of newspaper ads, something that was quite new at the time, the TikTok of its day, in drawing customers to their businesses.

As humorous and entertaining as I find the conclusion of *The Witches of New York*, I am also aware that Thomson was writing from a privileged, middle-class, male perspective. While the fortunes told to Thomson were reported as wildly inaccurate, and some of the fortune tellers even con-fessed (or were coerced into confessing) to being humbugs, Thomson missed a deeper and more interesting story. Living as a woman in the nineteenth century, particularly a poor one, was highly restrictive, and the female fortune tellers of the Lower East Side were living on the fringes of society. Whether they were widows, runaway single girls, or married women whose husbands had deserted them, they needed to eke out a liv-ing somehow. Fortune telling offered a relief from the restrictions imposed upon these women. They could decide how much to charge and who their customers were, they could stay home to work and keep an eye on their children or relatives if they needed to, and they were their own bosses.

Yes, they could be viewed as charlatans who made outrageous promises, but they were practicing this craft mainly because fortune telling was a rare and convenient way to survive. Genuine inquiry into the practice was reserved for those who could afford it.

For the clients who visited them, they offered a cheap form of entertainment, therapy, solace, and advice. Their services would become even more invaluable as the country commenced the Civil War. An estimated 620,000 soldiers would die between 1861 and 1865, and they would leave behind an even greater number of loved ones and family members who would grieve for them. After the war, the services of spiritualists and fortune tellers came into far higher demand.

Doesticks judged those he visited solely based on their differences from his life. He saw that they were poor and that they were women, and he was so blinded by these differences that he did not see the similarities. Essentially, they were charlatans and entertainers in their own way. Moreover, Thomson was more inclined to blame women in desperate circumstances, as they are easier to blame than the societal structures, forces, and institutions that created these circumstances.

Many customers on my tour are surprised to learn that fortune telling is a Class B misdemeanor in New York State. How can that be when there are so many storefront psychics in the city and a growth of fortune-telling services offered online? Well, one can legally perform fortune telling if notice is given that it is for "entertainment purposes only." And perhaps that is how we should view Doesticks's hyperbolic work about the fortune tellers of New York City in the nineteenth century: for entertainment purposes only.

Except that it wasn't entirely. As the *New York Daily Herald* wrote of Doesticks: "His peculiar drift of mind led him into comical idiosyncrasies of thought and criticism which caught the spirit of the age."[2] While the work of Doesticks fell into obscurity, he would continue to exert influence, including on Mark Twain, who mocked spiritualists in *The American Claimant* and in his "Schoolhouse Hill" version of his unfinished manuscript *The Mysterious Stranger*, and even Harry Houdini, who would expose the work of spiritualists during his career and owned a copy of Q. K. Philander Doesticks's *The Witches of New York*.

Epilogue: Ethel Parton

Lenormand Card: Clover (Meaning = *Hope*)

Let us end on a note of hope following a series of heartbreaking demises. We left the story of Mortimer Thomson and Grace Harrington Eldredge's daughter, Ethel Thomson, on December 1, 1862, the day she was born. When Ethel was only twelve days old, Grace died of scarlet fever, which she had caught from Mark Thomson. Mortimer was too devastated by his wife's death and busy with his career as a war correspondent to concern himself with his second child. From that point on, she was taken under the wing of her doting grandmother, Fanny Fern, and her husband, James Parton.

As a result, Ethel had a uniquely literary upbringing. In her early years, the family lived at 303 East Eighteenth Street in Manhattan, in the area known as Stuyvesant Square. Ethel recalled that while the nearby Gramercy Park was more exclusive, Stuyvesant Square was far more interesting, a place where she would call the sparrows to her and feed them with crumbs of stale bakers' rolls. The house belonged to Fern, and Ethel would crow about her grandmother's economic and critical success as a writer in a 1936 article in the *New Yorker*: "She was a columnist before columnists were heard of; her book 'Fern Leaves' and its successors were best-sellers before that term was invented."[1]

In the same article, Ethel wrote that her grandmother would usually think up her literary ideas while combing her hair or going for long, ambling walks through the city. In this three-story house was a parlor with sculptures of Goethe and Schiller in bronzed plaster. Ethel recounted knowing that they were poets and how to pronounce their names at a "small age." She described James Parton as a "born teacher" who served as Ethel's tutor in his book-lined study at the top of the house. She recollected being taken to an early revival of *The Black Crook,* considered the first American musical. The house was frequented by such esteemed visitors as Robert Bonner (the editor of the *Herald*), Horace Greeley (the founder and editor of the *New-York Tribune*), William Cullen Bryant (the poet and long-time editor of the *New York Evening Post*), and Thomas Nast.

Ethel also enjoyed the company of the female servants, who were a staple of her childhood home. Ethel wrote: "At 303, we employed occasional colored help—freed slaves, some of them—but usually our girls were Irish." Like some of Mortimer's fortune tellers, these women had hard lives and experienced little culture or delight. She wrote: "Our Irish girls were often just across, fresh from the pigs-in-the-parlor type of cabin of an Ireland happily fast receding into the past, and they had had little or no training to fit them for a civilized kitchen." However, Ethel was sympathetic toward the servants, and she wrote of reading to and writing letters for them. She found value in their stories. Sometimes, when she visited the kitchen, she "picked up first-hand stories of slave days in the South, Irish village life, Irish fairy lore, and the tragedy of Irish famines."[2]

The Irish Potato Famine had occurred just over twenty years before the time of Ethel's article, and it led to a flood of Irish immigration to the United States. Irish labor was widely available and inexpensive. The work of an Irish maid was brutally hard, involving long hours and heavy lifting. The maids would rise each morning well before the family they served, light fires, cook breakfast, clean dishes, scrub floors on their hands and knees, hand wash and iron clothes, fetch coal to keep the family warm, and heft it up and down stairs. They worked up to sixteen hours a day and earned approximately $1 to $1.25 per week plus board.[3] It is likely these kinds of hardships that the fortune tellers were trying to avoid.

But Ethel's life was nothing like the lives of her servants. She enjoyed taking in the sights of the city, awestruck by the looming structure of the Croton Distributing Reservoir on Forty-Second Street and Fifth Avenue, with its fifty-foot-high granite walls and towering Egyptian façade. Or she would frolic in Central Park with the menagerie animals. She also enjoyed the shop windows of department stores such as Lord & Taylors, Arnold, Constable, and, most of all, A.T. Stewart. She took excursions to Brentano's bookstore on Twenty-Seventh Street and Fifth Avenue with James Parton. While he examined French and English books, she would browse the children's department, where she perhaps first gleaned ideas for her future tales: "Except for occasional excursions into fairy tales, I wanted stories of action and excitement," she wrote. "The African adventures of Paul du Chaillu with pigmies, witch doctors, and gorillas were prime favorites; and the first lecture I ever attended was by the gay and gallant little Frenchman."[4]

More adventures abounded when Parton took Ethel to the food markets of New York City, where they would try such exotic delicacies as venison, prairie-chicken, guavas, pomegranates, fresh coconuts with milk in them, sea turtle, and bear steak.

One day, Ethel recollected, she found her pet canary, "a sweet singer," dead in its cage, having been devoured by a rat that had forced its way through the wires. After a morning of sobbing into soft pillows, Parton took her for a walk to the Clarendon Hotel on Eighteenth Street and Fourth Avenue, where he ordered an omelet with truffles to comfort them both. Ethel had not had truffles before, and James carefully explained to her that they were an underground mushroom that could only be discovered by pigs that hunted for them, which filled Ethel with wonder. She wrote:

> He made such a fascinating story out of truffle-hunting that by the time the truffles arrived, I was more than willing to let him put some on my plate to try . . . and some omelet, too, because truffles weren't meant to eat alone, and wouldn't taste right. . . . Together, they tasted quite right and very delicious. He was able to bring me back to a worried family, fed, composed and fairly cheerful, ready to carry on once more in a cruel world.[5]

In the same essay, Ethel expounded:

> There could scarcely have been a household composed of three more ardent child-lovers than my grandmother, "Fanny Fern" Parton, once-famous columnist, her husband, James Parton, biographer and essayist, and her daughter by a first marriage, Ellen Eldredge. They devoted themselves with equal assiduity and affection to the upbringing of the frail baby left in their care by the death of my young mother.[6]

Clearly adored by Fern and Parton, Ethel seemed to be doted upon the most by her grandmother. In the book *Eminent Women of the Age*, Grace Greenwood quoted Fern's words regarding the granddaughter she affectionately called Effie, "*She* is my poem."[7] Fern had also once written, "I think there is nothing on earth so lovely as the first waking of a little child in the morning. The gleeful, chirping voice. The bright eye. . . . The perfect happiness—the perfect faith in all future to-morrows!"[8]

Ethel heard little from her father, Mortimer Thomson.[9] The scholar Daniel Fletcher Slater wrote his dissertation on Thomson in the 1930s and corresponded with Ethel while researching it. In her letters, Ethel recollected her father wearing a Scotch cap and that he had "a way though I was quite a big girl, of snatching me up cyclonically and holding me high in the air." Thomson never wrote his daughter letters but would visit the family at their Stuyvesant Square home, often with his son Mark, whom Ethel described as "a very handsome little fellow, shy and quiet but manly, and strongly resembling his father."[10]

Despite having little contact with her father, he stoked Ethel's imagination in her golden years. Her 1937 children's book *Vinny Applegay: A Story of the 1870's*, is heavily based on her childhood growing up in Stuyvesant Square. The protagonist, Vinny, is cared for by two uncles, one of whom had a story from the Civil War Draft Riots that may sound a little familiar:

"It happened that Zinny was on the street the first day; on Second Avenue, close to Stuyvesant Square; and in the square a gang of howling half-grown boys, with a few older toughs and pug-uglies among them, was fast becoming a real mob. They caught sight of Zinny, just as she was making for a side street."

"This one?" asked Vinny.

"This one, yes. They set up a mad yell. The few who could get hold of a stone or a brick hurled it after her, and in an instant they were hot on her heels. She's old and rheumatic. She couldn't run. It looked like the end, for her; it would have been, if Drum hadn't come along, just arrived from the front for a few days' furlough. He held them off at the point of his pistol with brickbats flying around his head, while she climbed the stoop."

"Ours?" asked Vinny.

"Ours, yes. He backed up slowly after her himself; he had to keep his face to the mob, or they'd have been on him like a pack of wolves. I was there to let them in, and bolt the door, and the worst was over. But Drum stood in that window over there, with his pistol ready till the yelling died down and at last the crowd broke up and drifted away. If he hadn't, somebody might have climbed in from the stoop; there was a ledge above the basement, and from the stoop a nimble fellow could do it easily. One bold rascal tried to, but a shot in the air was enough, and he scrambled back in a hurry. They weren't the stuff to face bullets."

"And you saved Zinny's life with a pistol, and then said there wasn't any story," said Vinny reproachfully, addressing the widespread sheet of the Times, her eyes shining. "Oh, Uncle Drum!"[11]

Clearly, someone had told Ethel the story of her father's heroics, and she used that dramatic moment in her novel. Besides this scene, Ethel would occasionally use her father's behavior as inspiration for other characters, such as Simeon Thripp in her novel *Penelope Ellen*, as well as other itinerant, irresponsible characters.

Occasionally, the idyllic spell of the House of Fern and Parton was broken, as it was the target of numerous robberies of silver and jewelry, according to Ethel, including a particularly dangerous one in which the criminals had been living in the house for a week while the family was out of town. Ethel had gone upstairs to retrieve some item and was unable to open the closet door. The robbers were apparently hiding in the closet and bracing the doorknob against Ethel's attempted turns.

Summers spent in the countryside were a staple of Ethel's childhood. The family variously spent summers in Brattleboro and Highgate Springs in Vermont and Orchard Beach in Maine. For the last six years of her life, Fern was battling cancer, and she finally succumbed on October 10, 1872. On November 2 that year, the fourth page of the *New York Ledger*, where Fern's column was usually printed, was edged in black, to commemorate her significant contributions to the newspaper. She was buried in Mount Auburn Cemetery in Cambridge, Massachusetts, beside her first husband, Charles Eldredge.

Around the time of her grandmother's death, reports of the demise of Ethel's father were reaching her family. In a letter from James Parton to Ellen Eldredge in 1873, he wrote of putting Thomson in an institution and further wrote, "Be sure, when this has blown by to destroy that letter for Effie's sake. She must *never* know of these things."[12] In another letter which he addressed to both Ellen and Ethel in 1875, he would answer their inquiries after Mortimer but also admit to both that Ethel's father was seriously ill: "I met Mortimer in the street yesterday. He, too, has been, and is, very sick—enough for four months. His appearance and voice are much changed, and, indeed, he looks to me much like one who is fatally diseased."[13]

Her father died in 1875, and there is no record of Ethel having attended the funeral. It is not known what she was told about his death.

James Parton had just joined Ethel and Ellen at Newburyport and was remodeling the house where they would all live.

When Fanny Fern passed away, it would not have been considered appropriate at that time for a middle-aged man to be living with two young ladies. Ellen was in her late twenties, and Ethel was barely in her teens. As a result, Ellen needed to move from New York, and she wanted to bring up Ethel in a small town. She was also eager to get away from relatives and New York society, who had made their disapproval of her mother very clear and extended that condemnation to Ellen.

James had encountered the idyllic town of Newburyport, Massachusetts, earlier in his life while researching his biography of General Benjamin F. Butler. He had been sailing with Butler on his yacht, *America*, when he and the other guests went ashore for three days of calm. There he saw Newburyport for the first time and fell in love with it. At his suggestion, Ellen and Ethel moved there, while he remained in New York City. He visited them in Newburyport often. Ethel continued her literary life, socializing with relatives of the poet John Greenleaf Whittier, as well as other prominent Newburyport families who told her stories handed down through the generations. This would later have an enormous influence on Ethel's literary career.

Two years after Ellen and Ethel moved to Newburyport, Ellen wrote to James that they would have to move into a different boarding house. James, who delighted in his visits to Newburyport to see Ethel and Ellen, decided to move to be with them. In February 1875, he bought a clapboard house at 270 High Street and moved in on May Day, 1875. Ethel and Ellen moved in with him.

An affection began to grow between James and Ellen. This might seem shocking now (and it was shocking to some back then), but other accounts leading up to the marriage indicated that they wanted to be together for the sake of Ethel. On February 3, 1876, they were wed quietly in Newburyport at their home, with a few friends in attendance. Once word got out in the newspapers, however, it created quite a stir, as can be seen in this nasty letter that appeared several weeks following the marriage:

Mrs. Burnham writes from New York to the St. Louis *Republican*: "Fanny Fern" must have flopped over in her grave last Sunday night, when her daughter married her husband. Fanny had two very fat, plain girls, always her constant companions. The one married Mortimer Thomson (Doesticks), and died the first or second year thereafter, leaving a nice little girl who must be now fifteen years old.

The other was an old maid who after her mother's death, took care of the child and her stepfather. Now she goes off to Massachusetts and marries her pop. My gracious! What a people! All the little details were attended to. Nothing seems to have been omitted except a casual glance at the statutes of the State. Fanny's daughter was a remarkably plain girl, but I should suppose she might have found someone outside her immediate family. Go on James, and while you fix up the statute, make it lawful to marry your wife's granddaughter, for there's little Miss Thomson coming up; you may want to marry her in a year or so.[14]

However, a rebuttal to this thinking, defending the marriage of James and Ellen, appeared in the *Star Tribune*:

In the present instance it was most natural that James Parton and Ellen Eldredge should be married. She was the daughter of Fanny Fern, who also the wife of James Parton. Her elder sister was married to Mortimer Thomson; but, dying a year after her marriage, left a daughter in the care of her sister Ellen and her mother, Mrs. Parton. This daughter was the idol of Fanny Fern's household, worshipped equally by herself and daughter and Mr. Parton. Fanny dying, the child became the special charge of Miss Eldredge and Mr. James Parton, and to her education and development they have devoted their lives. Neither has apparently had any other ambition than to secure the welfare and happiness of this orphan child.[15]

The letter was signed "A Friend," but a note underneath the letter in parentheses stated it was probably written by Colonel Clifford Thomson.[16]

It turns out the marriage was considered illegal in Massachusetts. A week following their first wedding, James and Ellen went to New York City on February 10, 1876, to be wed a second time in a state where their union was considered legal. James did petition the General Court of Massachusetts to recognize their first marriage in the aftermath, but while the bill passed almost unanimously in the Senate and by a good majority in the House, it was vetoed by Governor Rice on the grounds that its passage would be "contrary to principles of legislation and the good of society."[17]

Although Ethel was not legally adopted, she changed her name from Grace Ethel Thomson to Ethel Parton in January 1884.[18] A date was set of the fourth Monday of January for anyone to show cause that the name change not be granted, and Ethel was requested to print three notifications of the citation in the newspaper for three weeks in a row, which she did.

James and Ellen would have two children together, Mabel (born 1877) and Hugo (born 1879). In the same year that Hugo was born, James read a shocking notice in the *Tribune* regarding Clifford Thomson's only son, Clifford Lincoln, stating that he had drowned at the age of eleven on July 5. The news also upset Ethel and moved James to write a note to Clifford expressing his distress and condolences. "How can you bear it?" James asked. "To cherish hopes for so many years and then see them come to naught! There is only one consolation, and that is, that he is safe. Nothing can touch him further." Toward the end of his letter he wrote, "I never saw Effie so overwhelmed as she was when she saw that paper."[19]

Perhaps it was her distress in response to Clifford Lincoln's drowning that caused James to keep the true circumstances of her half-brother Mark's death from her. In corresponding with Daniel Fletcher Slater regarding Mark's death, Ethel had written that he "died of pneumonia, among strangers, at twenty six."[20] However, according to a report in the *Billings Gazette* on November 9, 1885, Mark had been in Butte, Montana, when he was assaulted by robbers, who stole a "large sum of money" from him. He was lying in a hospital, in "a precarious condition,"[21] when he was joined by Paul Ledyard Van Cleve, his uncle on his mother's side, who came from Townsend, Montana. There were hopes of Mark's recovery, but by November 14, 1885, he was reported dead. Mark is buried in Mount Mariah Cemetery in Butte, Montana.

In 1886, James bought a larger house in Newburyport at 272 High Street, just across from their former home, though he kept 270 High Street. While in his final years James was said to be mentally alert and continued writing, he was suffering from a weak heart and was quietly aware of his deterioration. Ethel recollected how one night, just a few weeks before his death, she was reading Frank Stockton's story "The Squirrel Inn" to the family, and while it was an amusing piece, James was too tired to listen and drifted off to sleep. A sad silence hung over the household. On October 17, 1891, he passed away in his sleep at the age of sixty-nine. He left everything to Ellen and Ethel.

James had been anxious for Ellen's and Ethel's future. Recognizing Ethel's innate literary talent, he encouraged her to pursue a writing career following his death. In the fall of 1891, when she was twenty-eight years old, Ethel debuted as a writer in *New England Magazine*, a monthly literary magazine published in Boston, from 1884 to 1917. Her twenty-three-page illustrated article documented the native and colonial history of Newburyport and eventual growth to the thriving town it was in her time. She also touched upon the town's brush with witch trials. Newburyport's witch was Goody Morse, who was tried and sentenced to death several years before the outbreak of witchcraft accusations in Salem. Goody Morse had a devoted husband. His persistence led to her reprieve, and she was eventually set free.

This writing debut was a triumph, and Ethel enjoyed other publishing successes in such magazines as the *New Yorker, Horn Book, St. Nicholas Magazine*, the "For Every Boy and Girl" section of the *Oklahoma City Times*, and the *Record Argus*, among others. Moreover, she was on the staff of the *Youth's Companion* for forty years, the magazine started by her great-grandfather Nathaniel Willis. The *Youth's Companion* was an American children's magazine founded in 1827. It was published for over one hundred years, until it was merged with the *American Boy* in 1929. The Youth's Companion Building in Boston is now on the National Register of Historic Places. Ethel even had publications of her own in the *Youth's Companion*, including the stories "Susan Tongs" and "An Afternoon in Rome."

In 1900, Ellen sold the large house at 272 High Street and moved back to 270 High Street. Ethel lived with Ellen until she passed away in 1922. She called Ellen her "Auntie-Mama." Ethel inherited 270 High Street from Ellen but sold it in 1935, as she could no longer afford to live there. She moved to a lodging house not too far away at 104 High Street.

Perhaps because of her upbringing by Fanny Fern or because she herself was an independent woman, it may come as no surprise that Ethel was a suffragette. In 1915, she wrote a letter to the editor of a local newspaper expressing her support for women's suffrage, and it was reported that she had joined a local women's march in Boston advocating for the same issue. She kept her suffrage parade ribbon for her entire life, and it can still be viewed in the Ethel Parton archives at Smith College. It is interesting to imagine the conversations she may have had with her father had he lived longer, given his hostile writing regarding women's rights.

After years of publishing short pieces in literary and children's magazines, as well as editing the *Youth's Companion*, Ethel began publishing children's books. Her novels were mainly set in historic times at various points in the 1800s and in Newburyport, except for *Vinny Applegay*, which was set in 1870s New York. In 1931, when she was sixty-nine years old, her first book, *Melissa Ann: A Girl of the 1820s*, was published. This was followed by eight more books, which were published until 1945, just after she died. Her final book was *The Year without a Summer: A Story of 1816*. The books were lauded in the press.

The *New York Times* published a review from Ethel's peer, the children's book author and librarian Anne T. Eaton, who loved Ethel's novel

Penelope Ellen and Her Friends: Three Little Girls of 1840, published by Viking Press in 1936.

> Not only the three little girls in the story of Penelope Ellen and her friends, but the older people as well, are convincing. In Grandma Pidgen Miss Parton has drawn a charming portrait of a delightfully independent old lady with a sense of humor. It is of value to children to read of a society where the importance of boys and girls is not overemphasized, and Penelope Ellen and her playmates seem all the more real to child readers when seen against a background of sensible and kindly grown-ups.[22]

The same paper also praised Ethel's *The House Between: A Story of the 1850's*: "Lifelike, spiced with humor, and written with fine integrity, Miss Parton's six books are a splendid contribution to the stories about this country which give to American boys and girls a deeper understanding of their heritage."[23] Ethel became a celebrity in Newburyport beyond the fame that came from being raised by Fanny Fern and James Parton. The Newburyport Public Library, for example, hosted an eightieth birthday celebration in her honor and following her passing would issue a bookplate featuring Ethel's illustrated portrait for the Ethel Parton Memorial Fund.

Ethel died in the Anna Jacques Hospital at the age of eighty-two in 1944. She had sustained injuries after falling the week before and was unable to recover. In her obituaries, it was noted her only survivors were her brother, Hugo Parton; a nephew, Major James Parton, US Army; and a niece, Niké Parton, who was serving with the Women's Auxiliary Corps but would later go on to become a prominent Florida artist.

What emerges from Ethel's life is that options and opportunities were slowly changing for women, paved by the likes of Fanny Fern, the investigative journalist Nellie Bly, and the book reviewer Margaret Fuller. The life of a woman and storyteller did not need to be one of impoverishment, as it might have been for fortune tellers of the past. Nor did a woman's fate have to be one of marriage. Expectations and possibilities were changing; marriage and children were not among the very slender options available to women like Ethel Parton and perhaps some of the fortune tellers who had been visited by Doesticks.

ACKNOWLEDGMENTS

Many articles used for researching *Mortimer and the Witches* were retrieved from Newspapers.com and the *New York Times'* Time Machine archives. The Vault at Pfaff's organized by Lehigh University, available online, provided invaluable information regarding Thomson and his associates. Lehigh University also provided crucial research, making the Thomas Butler Gunn diaries available online in the initial part of writing this book. Volumes 16–24 are now accessible at Missouri Digital Heritage, maintained by the Missouri History Museum.

Special thanks are due to the archivists at Houghton Library at Harvard University, where James Parton's papers are kept. Sharon Spieldenner at Newburyport Public Library Archival Center was extremely helpful in locating research materials for Ethel Parton.

At Smith College's Special Collections, Fanny Fern's and Ethel Parton's papers were a treasure trove of information, with particular thanks to Mary Biddle for her assistance. The New York Public Library's digital archive system has scans of the *New-York Tribune* and New York City directories that proved valuable to my research. Their papers on Charles Anderson Dana also contributed to this research. Thank you to Eirini Melena Karoutsos and Marcia Kirk at the Municipal Archives for all their helpful input on police and court records. The New-York Historical Society holds the papers of Clifford Thomson, which contained fascinating letters, photographs, and booklets that helped illuminate the life of Mortimer Thomson. Thank you to the University of Michigan for going above and beyond, sending me numerous PDFs pertaining to Thomson's time as an undergraduate student and more. The Minnesota Historical Society shared PDF copies of correspondence between Mortimer Thomson and Anna Van Cleve. I am indebted to Sara Durkacs and Jhon Usmanov for searching the archives of Green-Wood Cemetery for me and helping solve the mystery of Thomson's death.

Cemeteries visited included Green-Wood Cemetery in Brooklyn, New York (Mortimer Thomson, Anna Van Cleve, Grace Eldredge, Sophia Thomson, Edwin Thomson); Mount Auburn Cemetery in Cambridge, Massachusetts (Fanny Fern); Oak Hill Cemetery in Newburyport, Massachusetts (James Parton, Ethel Parton, Ellen Willis Eldredge); and Holy Sepulchre Cemetery in East Orange, New Jersey (Clifford Thomson).

The podcasts *The Bowery Boys* and season two of *Unobscured* offered excellent insight into some of the themes covered in this book.

In the early stages of developing the book proposal, Roseanne Wells taught and offered helpful feedback at a Gotham Writers' Workshop online class, and I also received invaluable advice from Sarah Lohman and Brooke Borel at their nonfiction book proposal workshop through Brooklyn Brainery.

Extra-special thanks to my agent Eric Myers for recognizing the potential of and finding the right home for this manuscript.

Sangeeta Mehta has been a longtime friend and supporter who has given me excellent advice based on her years of experience in the publishing industry.

Thank you to Andrea Janes, founder of Boroughs of the Dead, for taking a chance on this story as a tour and always supporting the artistic endeavors of her guides. My fellow tour guide Silas Costello offered excellent comments and suggestions to strengthen this book.

Kambri Crews of Q.E.D. Astoria is such a wonderful advocate and cheerleader of artists and has always reacted with enthusiasm when I have proposed talks on weird and obscure topics to present at her venue, including this one. Thank you, Kambri, for hosting many of my events.

I was delighted when I found out someone was working on the biography of Mortimer Thomson's daughter, Ethel Parton, and I sought her out through social media. Sarah Jensen turned out to be a kindred spirit, and we had many exchanges about our research. Sarah also offered exceptional feedback and edits to the manuscript, and she was an enthusiastic cheerleader for this book. I was devastated when I learned she had passed away in December 2022, just as she was working on a book proposal for Ethel

Parton's biography. Sarah had spent years researching the book, and it is so deeply sad that she never got to finish it and share it with the world.

Thank you to Stacy Horn and Stephanie Azzarone for their detailed feedback on the book.

Thanks to Mauricio Merino for taking great author photos.

Many thanks to my patient editor, Fredric Nachbaur, and to all the staff at Fordham University Press for taking a chance on this book. Thank you to Rob Fellman for the detailed copyediting.

Finally, thank you to my mum and David for all their love and support over the years, and to my partner in life, Jeremy Diaz, for being my biggest champion in everything and keeping our household a joyous and creative one. Our feline familiars Elsa and Grayson make us laugh and coo daily, and my beloved companion of eighteen years, Grace, spent a great deal of time purring on my lap while the manuscript was in its preliminary stages.

NOTES

Introduction

1. I write of New York City as it was understood in the era when it was New Amsterdam, a colony of the Dutch, and later the New York City of the British. At this point, the city limits were below Chambers Street in Manhattan. S. R. Ferrara, *Accused of Witchcraft in New York* (History Press, 2023), is an excellent book that details witch trials that have taken place in the state of New York, including in the Bronx.

2. Christine Stansell, *City of Women: Sex and Class in New York, 1789–1860* (University of Illinois Press, 1987), 21.

3. Q. K. Philander Doesticks, *The Witches of New York* (T. B. Peterson and Brothers, 1858), 160.

4. James Dabney McCabe, *Secrets of the Great City* (Jones Brothers & Co., 1868), 337, https://archive.org/details/secretsofgreatcio1mcca.

5. Anonymous, *The Prophetess: Being the Life, Natural and Supernatural, of Mrs. B, Otherwise Known as Madame Rockwell, The Fortune-teller, for the Past Five Years at Barnum's City, in the City of New York* (J. S. Redfield, 1849), 7, 5, 9.

6. Doesticks, *The Witches of New York*, 340–41.

Chapter 1. Madame Morrow

1. Doesticks's article on Madame Morrow appeared in the *New-York Tribune* on February 13, 1857; and in Q. K. Philander Doesticks, *The Witches of New York* (T. B. Peterson and Brothers, 1858), chap. 6.

2. Doesticks, *The Witches of New York*, 132.

3. Doesticks, *The Witches of New York*, 133, 135.

4. Doesticks, *The Witches of New York*, 136.

5. Doesticks, *The Witches of New York*, 142.

6. Doesticks, *The Witches of New York*, 143.

7. Doesticks, *The Witches of New York*, 145.

8. Some records also note a date of 1832, but the most consistent and reliable year, including that on his tombstone and two census records, is 1831.

9. Fletcher Daniel Slater, "The Life and Letters of Mortimer Thomson," master's thesis, Northwestern University, 1931, 4, https://www.undercover.hosting.nyu.edu/s/undercover -reporting/item/14060. Slater also noted the common misspelling of Thomson's last name.

10. Slater, "The Life and Letters of Mortimer Thomson," 6.

11. Some newspapers wrote that Thomson's father was a physician, but they seem to be misinformed. The most reliable sources, such as Ethel Parton, Thomson's daughter, wrote several times that he was a lawyer, and his death certificate stated he was a lawyer.

12. Thomson's daughter Ethel Parton would write, "He [Clifford] and my father were extremely attached to one another." Letter of Ethel Parton to Daniel Fletcher Slater, July 20, 1931, Houghton Library, Harvard University.

13. "A Genial Soul," *The Inter Ocean*, July 1, 1875.

14. "Obituary. Mortimer Thomson—'Doesticks,'" *New York Times*, June 26, 1875.

15. "Q. K. Philander Doesticks, P.B.," *New York Herald*, June 26, 1875.

16. "Q. K. Philander Doesticks, P.B."

17. "Personal," *Burlington Daily Sentinel*, July 12, 1875.

18. "A Genial Soul."

19. "Who Is Doesticks?," *Evening Post*, November 18, 1854.

20. "Obituary. Mortimer Thomson—'Doesticks.'"

21. It has also been noted by the literary critic Fred Lorch that a young Samuel Clemens (aka Mark Twain) would have been setting type in the St. Louis *Evening News* office at the time. The editor there had been amused by and reprinted six of the Doesticks letters. Perhaps young Clemens recognized something of a kindred spirit in Doesticks, as they would later briefly correspond. Fred W. Lorch, "'Doesticks' and the Innocents Abroad," *American Literature* 20, no. 4 (January 1949): 446–47.

22. "Who's Doesticks," *Buffalo Daily Republic*, November 25, 1854.

23. "Doesticks Invents a Patent Medicine," *Detroit Daily Advertiser*, November 6, 1854.

24. "Fanny Fern," *Cahaba Gazette*, February 23, 1855.

25. "Our Literature," *Buffalo Commercial Advertiser*, February 23, 1855.

26. "Doesticks," *Buffalo Commercial Advertiser*, February 17, 1855.

27. "Q. K. Philander Doesticks, P.B.," *Vermont Journal*, February 23, 1855.

28. "Death of Mr. Mortimer Thomson," *New-York Tribune*, June 1, 1855.

29. "'Doesticks' Is Not Dead," *Times-Picayune*, June 9, 1855.

30. "'Doesticks' Says He Is Not Dead," *Raleigh Register*, June 23, 1855.

31. "Doesticks," *Living Age*, reprinted in *New England Farmer*, July 14, 1855.

32. "New Books," *Louisville Daily Courier*, July 14, 1855.

33. "Doesticks, What He Says," *Vermont Watchman and State Journal*, July 20, 1855.

34. "Doesticks: New York, Livermore," *The Citizen*, July 21, 1855.

35. Eddy Portnoy, "In the Palm of His Hand," *New York Jewish Week*, January 24, 2012, https://jewishweek.timesofisrael.com/in-the-palm-of-his-hand/.

36. Thomas Butler Gunn, *The Physiology of New York Boarding-Houses* (1857; Rutgers University Press, 2009), chap. 12, para. 11.

37. Gunn, *The Physiology of New York Boarding-Houses*, chap. 12, para. 11.

38. That estimate is likely bloated, as it would mean Madame Morrow would be seeing fifty to seventy-five customers a day.

39. Christine Stansell, *City of Women: Sex and Class in New York, 1789–1860* (University of Illinois Press, 1987), 114.

40. Fanny Fern, *Ruth Hall and Other Writings* (1855; Rutgers University Press, 1992), 96.

41. "Madame Morrow, Independent Clairvoyant," *Brooklyn Daily Eagle*, October 18, 1876.

42. When Westervelt was put on trial, it was also noted that Madame Morrow also went by the name Elizabeth Morris and that she sometimes lived in Philadelphia.

43. Cornelius Vanderbilt famously consulted with the spiritualist Victoria Woodhull and her sister Tennessee Claflin, with whom he was also having an affair.

Chapter 2. Madame Clifton

1. Doesticks's article on Madame Clifton appeared in the *New-York Tribune* on February 24, 1857; and in Q. K. Philander Doesticks, *The Witches of New York* (T. B. Peterson and Brothers, 1858), chap. 15.

2. Doesticks, *The Witches of New York*, 348–49.

3. Doesticks, *The Witches of New York*, 351.

4. Letter from Ethel Thomson to Daniel Fletcher Slater, July 26, 1931, Houghton Library, Harvard University.

5. Thomas Butler Gunn, *Thomas Butler Gunn Diaries*, vol. 9, transcript, October 24, 1858, The Vault at Pfaff's, Lehigh University, Bethlehem, PA, https://pfaffs.web.lehigh.edu /worksby/54227.

6. Gunn, *Thomas Butler Gunn Diaries*, vol. 11, November 13, 1859, https://pfaffs.web .lehigh.edu/worksby/54227.

7. Gunn, *Thomas Butler Gunn Diaries*, vol. 22, September 25, 1862, Missouri Digital Heritage, https://www.sos.mo.gov/mdh.

8. Gunn, *Thomas Butler Gunn Diaries*, vol. 7, December 30, 1855, https://pfaffs.web.lehigh .edu/worksby/54227.

9. Gunn, *Thomas Butler Gunn Diaries*, vol. 9, March 11, 1858, https://pfaffs.web.lehigh.edu /worksby/54227.

10. Gunn, *Thomas Butler Gunn Diaries*, vol. 10, July 10, 1859, https://pfaffs.web.lehigh.edu /worksby/54227.

11. "A Correction," *New-York Tribune*, March 2, 1857.

12. "The Witches of New-York No. X, Madame Clifton," *New-York Tribune*, February 24, 1857.

13. Anonymous, *The Gentleman's Directory [Applewood after Dark]* (1870), 9. From a copy in the collection of the New-York Historical Society.

14. "History," New York Academy of Medicine, https://www.nyam.org/about/history/.

15. "Bridget Tiernay Again in Trouble," *Memphis Daily Avalanche*, March 11, 1861.

16. "Sad Case of Persecution," *Memphis Daily Argus*, March 26, 1861.

Chapter 3. Madame Prewster

1. Doesticks's article on Madame Prewster appeared in the *New-York Tribune* on January 28, 1857; and in Q. K. Philander Doesticks, *The Witches of New York* (T. B. Peterson and Brothers, 1858), chap. 2.

2. Doesticks, *The Witches of New York*, 34.

3. Doesticks, *The Witches of New York*, 44.

4. Doesticks, *The Witches of New York*, 49.

5. Doesticks, *The Witches of New York*, 49.

6. "Doesticks Married," *Elwood Advertiser*, November 12, 1857; originally reported in *New Haven Palladium*, October 24, 1857.

7. Thomas Butler Gunn, *Thomas Butler Gunn Diaries*, vol. 9, transcript, November 15, 1857, The Vault at Pfaff's, Lehigh University, Bethlehem, PA, https://pfaffs.web.lehigh.edu /worksby/54227.

8. Gunn, *Thomas Butler Gunn Diaries*, vol. 9, November 13, 1857.

9. In a letter to Daniel Fletcher Slater, who was writing a thesis on the work of Mortimer Thomson, Thomson's daughter Ethel Parton would give further details of the friendship between Van Cleve and Eldredge: "Nanny Van Cleve was dark tiny exquisitely pretty and almost too shy to speak: she prompyly [*sic*] adored my tall and lovely mother with her golden hair, blue eyes and wild rose coloring. My mother was very kind to her and after her tragic death when Mark was born, she took a compassionate interest in the baby." Letter of Ethel Parton, July 20, 1931, Houghton Library, Harvard University.

10. "How Philander Doesticks Became a Broken-In Husband," *Polynesian*, May 22, 1858.

11. Gunn, *Thomas Butler Gunn Diaries*, vol. 9, February 24, 1858.

12. Michael Haines, "Fertility and Mortality in the United States," *EH*, https://eh.net /encyclopedia/fertility-and-mortality-in-the-united-states/.

13. Gunn, *Thomas Butler Gunn Diaries*, vol. 10, December 24, 1858.

14. Gunn, *Thomas Butler Gunn Diaries*, vol. 10, December 24, 1858.

15. Gunn, *Thomas Butler Gunn Diaries*, vol. 10, December 24, 1858.

16. Gunn, *Thomas Butler Gunn Diaries*, vol. 10, December 24, 1858.

17. J. Dixon Mann, *Forensic Medicine and Toxicology* (Charles Griffin, 1898), 102.

18. Onesipherous W. Bartley, *A Treatise on Forensic Medicine or Medical Jurisprudence* (Barry & Son, 1815), 43.

19. Charles Loring Brace, *The Dangerous Classes of New York and Twenty Years' Work among Them* (Wynkoop & Hallenbeck, 1872), chap. 10.

20. Christine Stansell, *City of Women: Sex and Class in New York, 1789–1860* (University of Illinois Press, 1987), 85.

21. Fanny Fern, *Ruth Hall and Other Writings* (1855; Rutgers University Press, 1992), 328.

22. Fern, *Ruth Hall and Other Writings*, 89–90.

23. "TO THE MAYOR F. WOOD," *Evansville Daily Journal*, February 15, 1855.

24. "A Raid among the Soothsayers," *New York Times*, November 23, 1855.

25. "A Raid among the Soothsayers."

26. "The New York Sorcerers," *New York Daily Herald*, October 23, 1858.

27. "Dr. Taylor's Balsam of Liverwort," *Commercial Advertiser and Journal*, August 16, 1841.

28. "The New York Sorcerers."

29. Fern, *Ruth Hall and Other Writings*, 327–28.

30. Brace, *The Dangerous Classes of New York*, chap. 3.

Chapter 4. Madame Widger

1. Doesticks's article on Madame Widger appeared in the *New-York Tribune* on January 23, 1857; and in Q. K. Philander Doesticks, *The Witches of New York* (T. B. Peterson and Brothers, 1858), chap. 4.

2. Doesticks, *The Witches of New York*, 83–85.

3. Doesticks, *The Witches of New York*, 87–88.

4. Doesticks, *The Witches of New York*, 95.

5. Doesticks, *The Witches of New York*, 96–97.

6. Doesticks, *The Witches of New York*, 97–98.

7. "The Witches of New York," *New England Farmer*, December 4, 1858.

8. "Few, Except Those Who Have Looked," *Baton Rouge Tri-Weekly Gazette and Comet*, January 9, 1859.

9. "Doesticks on Witches," *Times-Picayune*, December 14, 1858.

10. Ethel Parton, "Fanny Fern at the Hartford Female Seminary," *New England Magazine* 24 (March 1901): 98.

11. Letter from Harriett Beecher Stowe to James Parton, no date, Houghton Library, Harvard University.

12. Thomas Butler Gunn, *Thomas Butler Gunn Diaries*, vol. 8, transcript, June 1856, The Vault at Pfaff's, Lehigh University, Bethlehem, PA, https://pfaffs.web.lehigh.edu/worksby/54227.

13. Thomas Butler Gunn, *Thomas Butler Gunn Diaries*, vol. 9, June 20, 1858.

14. "It's So Easy," *Deseret News*, September 8, 1858.

15. "It's So Easy."

16. Thomas Butler Gunn, *Thomas Butler Gunn Diaries*, vol. 10, December 24, 1858.

17. Thomas Butler Gunn, *Thomas Butler Gunn Diaries*, vol. 10, May 31, 1859.

18. Thomas Butler Gunn, *Thomas Butler Gunn Diaries*, vol. 11, June 20, 1859.

19. Thomas Butler Gunn, *Thomas Butler Gunn Diaries*, vol. 11, July 17, 1859.

20. Thomas Butler Gunn, *Thomas Butler Gunn Diaries*, vol. 11, June 24, 1858.

21. P. B. Doesticks, Q.K., "Pluck, a Lecture," New-York Historical Society.

22. "Doesticks on 'Pluck.'" *New-York Tribune*, November 11, 1859.

23. Thomas Butler Gunn, *Thomas Butler Gunn Diaries*, vol. 11, November 13, 1859.

24. Thomas Butler Gunn, *Thomas Butler Gunn Diaries*, vol. 18, May 11, 1861, Missouri Digital Heritage, https://www.sos.mo.gov/mdh.

25. Thomas Butler Gunn, *Thomas Butler Gunn Diaries*, vol. 18, May 11, 1861, Missouri Digital Heritage, https://www.sos.mo.gov/mdh.

26. "Fanny Fern on Lovers and Marriageable Daughters," *New York Ledger*, March 30, 1861.

27. "The Vilest of Women," *New-York Tribune*, April 22, 1871.

28. "The Vilest of Women."

29. "The Vilest of Women."

30. "The Tribune's Expose of the Fortunetellers of New York," *Norfolk Virginian*, May 5, 1871.

31. Francesca Beauman, *Matrimony, Inc.: From Personal Ads to Swiping Right, a Story of America Looking for Love* (Pegasus, 2020), 92.

32. Quoted in Beauman, *Matrimony, Inc.*, 97.

33. "Matrimonial Advertisements," *New York Ledger*, January 3, 1857.

34. "A Fifteen-Year Old Husband," *Beatrice Weekly Express*, May 6, 1871.

35. "A Fifteen-Year Old Husband."

Chapter 5. Mr. Grommer

1. Doesticks's article on Mr. Grommer appeared in the *New-York Tribune* on May 9, 1857; and in Q. K. Philander Doesticks, *The Witches of New York* (T. B. Peterson and Brothers, 1858), chap. 14.

2. Doesticks, *The Witches of New York*, 309.

3. Doesticks, *The Witches of New York*, 314–15.

4. Doesticks, *The Witches of New York*, 319–20.

5. Doesticks, *The Witches of New York*, 326.

6. "American Civilization Illustrated: A Great Slave Auction," *New-York Tribune*, March 9, 1859.

7. "American Civilization Illustrated: A Great Slave Auction."

8. "American Civilization Illustrated: A Great Slave Auction."

9. A maker or repairer of casks and barrels.

10. "American Civilization Illustrated: A Great Slave Auction."

11. "American Civilization Illustrated: A Great Slave Auction."

12. "American Civilization Illustrated: A Great Slave Auction."

13. "American Civilization Illustrated: A Great Slave Auction."

14. Letter of Ethel Parton, July 20, 1931, Houghton Library, Harvard University.

15. Thomas Butler Gunn, *Thomas Butler Gunn Diaries*, vol. 10, transcript, March 16, 1859, The Vault at Pfaff's, Lehigh University, Bethlehem, PA, https://pfaffs.web.lehigh.edu /worksby/54227.

16. "A Special Messenger," *Richmond Dispatch*, March 12, 1859.

17. "Doesticks, an Abolitionist," *Athens Post*, April 8, 1859.

18. "Obituary. Mortimer Thomson—'Doesticks,'" *New York Times*, June 26, 1875. This is also confirmed in a letter from Ethel Parton: "The episode of the Draft Riots in New York city was one of the first that made any impression on me as a child, because the mob surged by our house an [*sic*] I used to be shown the empty space in the bricks where they tore up a sapling horse-chestnut for a club; also, how it was James Parton who saw the mob gathering for its attack on the Tribune office and left my grandmother alone in the riotous streets, at her urgency, while he hurried to carry them a warning, and then down to Governors Island to get troops; lastly, how my father found a terrified old negress pursued by howling rioters and backed her into a friendly doorway while he held them off at the point of a revolver." Letter of Ethel Thomson, August 1931, Houghton Library.

19. *New York City Directory*, 1869, Irma and Paul Milstein Division of United States History, Local History and Genealogy, New York Public Library, Digital Collections, https:// digitalcollections.nypl.org/items/050245b0-5374-0134-ac00-00505686a51c.

20. Leslie M. Harris, *In the Shadow of Slavery: African Americans in New York City, 1626–1863* (University of Chicago Press, 2004), 190.

21. "Slavers—and the Slave Trade," *Brooklyn Daily Eagle*, March 18, 1846.

22. Walt Whitman, *Walt Whitman's Selected Journalism* (University of Iowa Press, 2015), 52.

23. Maria Lydig Daly, *Diary of a Union Lady, 1861–1865* (Funk & Wagnalls, 1962), July 23, 1863.

Chapter 6. Mrs. Hayes

1. Q. K. Philander Doesticks, *The Witches of New York* (T. B. Peterson and Brothers, 1858), 172. Doesticks's article on Mrs. Hayes appeared in the *New-York Tribune* on February 25, 1857; and in Doesticks, *The Witches of New York*, chap. 8.

2. Doesticks, *The Witches of New York*, 181.

3. Doesticks, *The Witches of New York*, 182–83.

4. Charles Dickens, *American Notes* (Chapman & Hall, Ltd., 1913), https://www.gutenberg.org/files/675/675-h/675-h.htm.

5. Doesticks, *The Witches of New York*, 184.

6. Doesticks, *The Witches of New York*, 185.

7. Doesticks, *The Witches of New York*, 193.

8. "Doesticks Respectfully Inquireth: What Do the Women Want Us to Do about the War?" *Fremont Weekly Journal*, October 18, 1861.

9. "A Story of Doesticks," *Brooklyn Daily Eagle*, April 8, 1906.

10. Thomas Butler Gunn, *Thomas Butler Gunn Diaries*, vol. 18, transcript, August 6, 1861, Missouri Digital Heritage, https://www.sos.mo.gov/mdh.

11. "$5 Reward—Lost," *The Local News*, November 21, 1861.

12. "Death of Mortimer Thomson," *Marysville Daily Appeal*, July 7, 1875.

13. "Death of Clifford Thomson, Editor," *The Spectator*, October 3, 1912.

14. "A New Name for the War," *Buffalo Commercial*, February 11, 1862.

15. Thomas Butler Gunn, *Thomas Butler Gunn Diaries*, vol. 20, November 14, 1861.

16. "What Doesticks' Wife Wanted," *Saturday Evening Post*, December 14, 1861.

17. Thomas Butler Gunn, *Thomas Butler Gunn Diaries*, vol. 20, December 22, 1861.

18. Thomas Butler Gunn, *Thomas Butler Gunn Diaries*, vol. 22, September 24, 1862.

19. Thomas Butler Gunn, *Thomas Butler Gunn Diaries*, vol. 22, September 25, 1862.

20. Thomas Butler Gunn, *Thomas Butler Gunn Diaries*, vol. 23, October 3, 1862.

21. Thomas Butler Gunn, *Thomas Butler Gunn Diaries*, vol. 22, September 25, 1862.

22. Thomas Butler Gunn, *Thomas Butler Gunn Diaries*, vol. 23, October 19, 1862.

23. Thomas Butler Gunn, *Thomas Butler Gunn Diaries*, vol. 23, February 5, 1863.

24. Thomas Butler Gunn, *Thomas Butler Gunn Diaries*, vol. 24, April 4, 1863.

25. "An Offer," *Lancaster Gazette,* January 24, 1863.

26. "City Intelligence," *New York Daily Herald*, May 17, 1851.

27. "A Raid among the Soothsayers," *New York Times*, November 23, 1855.

28. "A Raid among the Soothsayers."

29. "A Raid among the Soothsayers."

30. "A Raid among the Soothsayers."

31. "A Raid among the Soothsayers."

Chapter 7. The Gipsy Girl

1. Doesticks's article on The Gipsy Girl appeared in the *New-York Tribune* on January 31, 1857; and in Q. K. Philander Doesticks, *The Witches of New York* (T. B. Peterson and Brothers, 1858), chap. 12.

2. Doesticks, *The Witches of New York*, 264.

3. Doesticks, *The Witches of New York*, 269.

4. Doesticks, *The Witches of New York*, 272–73.

5. Doesticks, *The Witches of New York*, 279.

6. Letter from Ethel Parton to Daniel Fletcher Slater, 1931, Houghton Library, Harvard University.

7. "Course of Lectures," *Quad-City Times*, November 12, 1859.

8. "Mortimer Thomson, Who Heard Henry Ward Beecher," *Democrat and Chronicle*, March 16, 1903.

9. Fletcher Daniel Slater, "The Life and Letters of Mortimer Thomson," master's thesis, Northwestern University, August 1931, 200, https://undercover.hosting.nyu.edu/files/original/45e12aeb77d42576e954e34109f1617c4a569324.pdf.

10. "American Humor and Humorists," *Brooklyn Daily Eagle*, September 9, 1865.

11. "Personal—Mr. Clifford Thomson," *Times Union*, July 15, 1865.

12. "Doesticks' Letters. Our New Post Mistress," *Street & Smith*, May 20, 1869.

13. Thomson spent more time with his son than his daughter. Corresponding with Daniel Fletcher Slater, who was writing a thesis about Thomson, Ethel Parton, Thomson's daughter, wrote a little more about the father/son relationship: "He used to come to see me in New York with my father, but not often enough for the usual brother and sisterly intimany [*sic*] to exist though we were fond enough of one another in a w[ay]. He was no [*sic*] brought up at Ann Arbor—if he was there at all as a boy it could not have been for long; and I don't think he was ever then. He was a very handsome little fellow, shy and quiet but manly and strongly resembling his father. I cannot give you his too brief or by dates or in detail. He was his fathers companion in New York; he was with relatives in Minnesota; he went to other relatives the Halls (of one of the famous old missionary families) in Honolulu." Letter from Ethel Parton to Daniel Fletcher Slater, July 20, 1931, Houghton Library.

14. "Doesticks' Letters. Doesticks on 'April Fooling,'" *Street & Smith*, May 13, 1869.

15. "Edwin Thompson, Esq.," *Yonkers Gazette*, March 28, 1868.

16. "Personal," *Star Tribune*, April 7, 1868.

17. "Mortimer Thomson, Known Familiarly as Doesticks," *Leavenworth Times*, October 13, 1869.

18. Letter reprinted in Fred W. Lorch, "'Doesticks' and Innocents Abroad," *American Literature* 20, no. 4 (January 1949): 447–48.

19. "A Talk about Josh Billings," *Redpath's Illustrated Weekly*, October 25, 1882.

20. "Personal," *Star Tribune*, June 6, 1872.

21. "Address and Poem," *Star Tribune*, September 14, 1872.

22. Slater, "The Life and Letters of Mortimer Thomson," vi.

23. "American Humorists of To-Day," *Rutland Daily Herald*, April 28, 1873.

24. "Mortimer Thomson, Better Known as 'Doesticks,'" *Star Tribune*, May 1, 1873.

25. "What Has Become of 'Doesticks?,'" *Idaho World*, September 26, 1874.

26. James Parton, letter to Ellen Eldredge, May 14, 1873, Houghton Library.

27. Mortimer Thomson, letter to Thurlow Weed, August 25, 1873, University of Rochester Library, Rochester, NY.

28. "Drunkenness a Disease—New Inebriate Asylum in New York," *Corvallis Gazette-Times*, February 13, 1869.

29. Rev. J. F. Richmond, *New York and Its Institutions, 1609–1873* (E. B. Treat, 1872), 558–59.

30. Richmond, *New York and Its Institutions*, 557.

31. "Charges against the New York Inebriate Asylum," *Baltimore Sun*, September 23, 1872.

32. "Is It a Failure?," *New York Times*, January 13, 1870.

33. "Wards Island Inebriate Asylum," *New York Times*, September 15, 1874.

34. "A Raid among the Soothsayers," *New York Times*, November 23, 1855.

35. "A Raid among the Soothsayers."

36. "An Officer of the Eighth Precinct," *New York Daily Herald*, March 30, 1871.

37. "Relief," *New York Daily Herald*, February 14, 1874.

Chapter 8. Mrs. Seymour

1. Q. K. Philander Doesticks, *The Witches of New York* (T. B. Peterson and Brothers, 1858), 204. Doesticks's article on Mrs. Seymour appeared in the *New-York Tribune* on February 6, 1857; and in Doesticks, *The Witches of New York*, chap. 9.

2. Doesticks, *The Witches of New York*, 206.

3. Doesticks, *The Witches of New York*, 208.

4. Doesticks, *The Witches of New York*, 210.

5. Tom Miller, "The J. E. Winterbottom Funeral Parlor—966 6th Avenue," *Daytonian in Manhattan*, January 25, 2020, http://daytoninmanhattan.blogspot.com/2020/01/the-j-e-winterbottom-funeral-parlor-966.html.

6. "The Funeral of 'Doesticks,'" *New York Herald*, June 28, 1875.

7. "We Read That Many Kind Friends of Poor Mortimer Thomson," *Buffalo Morning Express* and *Illustrated Buffalo Express*, June 30, 1875.

8. "A Brief History," Church of the Transfiguration, https://www.littlechurch.org/about/a-brief-history.

9. "James Parton," *Inter Ocean*, October 18, 1891.

10. "Mortimer Thomson, Who Heard Henry Ward Beecher," *Democrat and Chronicle*, March 16, 1903.

11. "The Clairvoyant Case—Sudden Death of Mr. Stuyvesant," *Washington Sentinel*, reprinted from *New York Herald*, December 11, 1853.

12. "Police Intelligence," *New York Daily Herald*, December 5, 1853.

13. "Clairvoyance," *Brooklyn Evening Star*, January 17, 1852.

14. "Police Intelligence."

15. George Templeton Strong, *The Diary of George Templeton Strong: The Turbulent Fifties, 1850–1859* (Macmillan, 1952), 321.

16. "The Bond Street Tragedy," *New York Herald*, February 5, 1857.

17. "Mrs. Seymour—A Clairvoyant in the Case," *New York Herald*, February 5, 1857.

18. "Arrest of New York Fortune Tellers," *Cleveland Daily Leader*, October 26, 1858.

19. "Mrs. Seymour, Clairvoyant," *New York Daily Herald*, March 6, 1871.

Concluding Remarks

1. Q. K. Philander Doesticks, *The Witches of New York* (T. B. Peterson and Brothers, 1858), 404–5.

2. "Mortimer Thomson," *New York Daily Herald*, June 26, 1875.

Epilogue. Ethel Parton

1. "A New York Childhood: The Seventies in Stuyvesant Square," *New Yorker*, June 13, 1936.

2. "A New York Childhood."

3. Alice Kessler-Harris, *Out to Work* (Oxford University Press, 2003), 55.

4. "A New York Childhood."

5. "A Little Girl and Two Authors," *The Horn Book* 17, no. 2 (March–April 1941): 86.

6. "A Little Girl and Two Authors."

7. James Parton, *Eminent Women of the Age: Being Narratives of the Lives and Deeds of the Most Prominent Women of the Present Generation* (1869; HardPress, 2018), chap. 3.

8. "A Child's Mission," *New York Ledger*, March 23, 1867.

9. When corresponding with Slater regarding her upbringing, Ethel had written, "Few children, I gratefully believe, ever had a happier childhood than I. James Parton, no kin to me by blood, loved me as his own from the moment, I have been told, when my baby fingers seized his and I gave him my first smile. My grandmother Fanny Fern Parton while she lived and my Aunt Ellen from my birth to her death at nearly eighty, so nested me in love and care that I was I suppo [*sic*] one of the few motherless and practically fatherless children who never for an instant of her life missed either father or mother. My own father I knew too little to love; I welcomed his rare visits as those of a special and exciting visitor, but he had no real part in my life." Letter of Ethel Parton, August 1931, Houghton Library, Harvard University.

10. Fletcher Daniel Slater, "The Life and Letters of Mortimer Thomson," master's thesis, Northwestern University, August 1931, 209, https://undercover.hosting.nyu.edu/files/original /45e12aeb77d42576e954e34109f1617c4a569324.pdf. Photographs of Mark in the Fanny Fern and Ethel Parton Collection of Smith College also convey that father and son were the spitting image of each other.

11. Ethel Parton, *Vinny Applegay: A Story of the 1870's* (Viking, 1937), 113–14.

12. James Parton, letter to Ellen Eldredge, n.d., Houghton Library.

13. Letter from James Parton, February 4, 1875, Houghton Library.

14. "Parton's Wife," *Kansas Daily Tribune*, February 26, 1876.

15. "James Parton's Marriage," *Star Tribune*, February 13, 1876.

16. James Parton and Clifford Thomson stayed in touch following Thomson's death. Thomson had also sent a letter to Parton offering support for the marriage. "I see by the papers that you and Nelly have at last gone through with the very sensible ceremony which makes you man and wife—the blue laws of the state of Massachusetts sells to the contrary notwithstanding. I congratulate you both most heartily, and hope your life may be prosperous and happy." Letter from Clifford Thomson to James Parton, February 11, 1876, Houghton Library.

17. Milton E. Flower, *James Parton: The Father of Modern Biography* (Greenwood, 1968), 171.

18. Her court petition was reported in the *Newburyport Daily Herald*, January 14, 1884.

19. Letter to Clifford Thomson, July 11, 1879, New-York Historical Society.

20. Letter from Ethel Parton to Daniel Fletcher Slater, July 20, 1931, Houghton Library.

21. "Mark Thompson's [*sic*] Many Friends," *Billings Gazette*, November 9, 1885.

22. "The New Books for Boys and Girls," *New York Times*, March 22, 1936.

23. "Old Newburyport," *New York Times*, May 2, 1943.

BIBLIOGRAPHY

Anbinder, Tyler. *City of Dreams: The Four-Hundred-Year Epic History of Immigrant New York.* Mariner Books, 2017.

Anstice, Rev. Henry. *History of St. George's Church in the City of New York, 1752–1811–1911.* Harper & Brothers, 1911.

Anonymous. *The Gentleman's Directory [Applewood after Dark],* 1870. From a copy in the New-York Historical Society.

Anonymous. *The Prophetess: Being the Life, Natural and Supernatural, of Mrs. B, Otherwise Known as Madame Rockwell, the Fortune-teller, for the Past Five Years at Barnum's City, in the City of New York.* J. S. Redfield, 1849.

Anonymous. *The Life and Beauties of Fanny Fern.* T. B. Peterson, 1855.

Applegate, Debby. *The Most Famous Man in America: The Biography of Henry Ward Beecher.* Image, 2007.

Baics, Gergely. *Feeding Gotham: The Political Economy and Geography of New York, 1790–1860.* Princeton University Press, 2016.

Bartley, Onesipherous W. *A Treatise on Forensic Medicine or Medical Jurisprudence.* Barry & Son, 1815.

Beauman, Francesca. *Matrimony Inc.: From Personal Ads to Swiping Right, a Story of America Looking for Love.* Pegasus, 2020.

Bly, Nellie. *Ten Days in a Mad-House: The Original 1887 Edition (Nellie Bly's Experience on Blackwell's Island).* 1887; electronic repr. 2021.

Bourke, Joanna. *Rape: Sex Violence History.* Counterpoint, 2007.

Brace, Charles Loring. *The Dangerous Classes of New York and Twenty Years' Work Among Them.* Wynkoop & Hallenbeck, 1872.

Braude, Ann. *Radical Spirits: Spiritualism and Women's Rights in Nineteenth-Century America.* Indiana University Press, 2001.

Browder, Clifford. *The Wickedest Woman in New York: Madame Restell, the Abortionist.* Archon, 1988.

Browne, Junius Henri. *The Great Metropolis: A Mirror of New York*. 1869; HardPress, 2017.

Burrows, Edwin G., and Mike Wallace. *Gotham: A History of New York City to 1898*. Oxford University Press, 1999.

Carpenter, Teresa, ed. *New York Diaries, 1609 to 2009*. Modern Library, 2012.

Crane, Stephen. *Maggie: A Girl of the Streets*. Digireads.com, 2009.

Daly, Maria Lydig. *Diary of a Union Lady, 1861–1865*. Funk & Wagnalls, 1962.

DeBow, J. D. B. *Statistic View of the United States, Embracing Its Territory, Population—White, Free Colored, and Slave—Moral and Social Condition, Industry, Property, and Revenue: The Detailed Statistics of Cities, Towns and Counties; Being a Compendium of the Seventh Census, to Which Are Added the Results of Every Previous Census, Beginning with 1790, in Comparative Tables, with Explanatory and Illustrative Notes, Based upon the Schedules and Other Official Sources of Information*. B. Tucker, Senate printer, 1854.

DeVillo, Stephen Paul. *The Bowery: The Strange History of New York's Oldest Street*. Skyhorse, 2017.

Dickens, Charles. *American Notes*. 1842. https://www.cmadras.com/136/136j1.pdf.

Doesticks, Q. K. Philander. *Doesticks What He Says: Containing the Whole of His Celebrated and Original Letters*. Edward Livermore, 1855.

———. "Pluck: A Lecture." Printed by Clifford Thomson for private circulation only, 1883. Retrieved from the archives of the New-York Historical Society.

———. *The Witches of New York*. T. B. Peterson and Brothers, 1858.

Doesticks, Q. K. Philander, et al. *What Became of the Slaves on a Georgia Plantation?: Great Auction Sale of Slaves, at Savannah, Georgia, March 2d & 3d. A Sequel to Mrs. Kemble's Journal*. S.l.: s.n, 1863. http://www.loc.gov/item/11003986/.

Fair, Susan. *American Witches: A Broomstick Tour through Four Centuries*. Skyhorse, 2016.

Faust, Drew Gilpin. *This Republic of Suffering: Death and the American Civil War*. Vintage, 2008.

Feder, Fred. *Lessons from the Past: Journalists' Lives and Work, 1830–1950*. Waveland, 2000.

Feldman, Benjamin. *Butchery on Bond Street: Sexual Politics and the Burdell-Cunningham Case in Antebellum New York*. Wanderer, 2018.

Fern, Fanny. *Fern Leaves from Fanny's Port-folio*. 1854; Hard Press, 2017.

———. *Ginger-Snaps*. Carleton, Publisher, Madison Square, 1870.

———. *Ruth Hall and Other Writings*. 1855; Rutgers University Press, 1992.

Ferrara, Eric. *The Bowery: A History of Grit, Graft, and Grandeur*. History Press, 2019.

Ferrara, S. R. *Accused of Witchcraft in New York*. History Press, 2023.

Fitzharris, Lindsey. *The Butchering Art: Joseph Lister's Quest to Transform the Grisly World of Victorian Medicine*. Scientific American/Farrar, Straus & Giroux, 2017.

Flower, Milton E. *James Parton: The Father of Modern Biography*. Greenwood, 1968.

Gabriel, Mary. *Notorious Victoria: The Uncensored Life of Victoria Woodhull—Visionary, Suffragist, and First Woman to Run for President*. Algonquin, 1998.

Goldsmith, Barbara. *Other Powers: The Age of Suffrage, Spiritualism, and the Scandalous Victoria Woodhull*. Knopf, 2011.

Gunn, Thomas Butler. *The Physiology of New York Boarding-Houses*. 1857; Rutgers University Press, 2009.

———. *Thomas Butler Gunn Diaries*. Retrieved from Lehigh University website, https://pfaffs .web.lehigh.edu/worksby/54227; and Missouri Digital Heritage website, https://www.sos. mo.gov/mdh.

Hagen, Carrie. *We Is Got Him: The Kidnapping That Changed America*. Abrams, 2011.

Harris, Leslie M. *In the Shadow of Slavery: African Americans in New York City, 1626–1863*. University of Chicago Press, 2004.

Hartman, Saidiya. *Wayward Lives, Beautiful Experiments: Intimate Histories of Riotous Black Girls, Troublesome Women, and Queer Radicals*. Norton, 2020.

Hauck-Lawson, Annie, and Jonathan Deutsch. *Gastropolis: Food and New York City*. Columbia University Press, 2008.

Headley, Joel T. *The Great Riots of New York, 1712–1873*. 1873; Cosimo Classics, 2009.

Hemstreet, Charles. *Literary New York: Its Landmarks and Associations*. Knickerbocker, 1903.

Horn, Stacy. *Damnation Island: Poor, Sick, Mad, and Criminal in Nineteenth-Century New York*. Algonquin Books of Chapel Hill, 2018.

Jones, Jacqueline. *Saving Savannah: The City and the Civil War*. Vintage, 2008.

Kang, Lydia, MD, and Nate Petersen. *Quackery: A Brief History of the Worst Ways to Cure Everything*. Workman, 2017.

Kemble, Frances Anne. *Journal of a Residence on a Georgian Plantation in 1838–1839*. University of Georgia Press, 1984.

Kessler-Harris, Alice. *Out to Work*. Oxford University Press, 2003.

Kurlansky, Mark. *The Big Oyster: History on the Half Shell*. Random House, 2007.

Landon, Melville D. (Eli Perkins). *Kings of the Platform and Pulpit*. Werner Company, 1900.

Mann, J. Dixon, *Forensic Medicine and Toxicology*. Charles Griffin, 1898.

Martin, Justin. *Rebel Souls: Walt Whitman and America's First Bohemians*. Da Capo, 2014.

McCabe, James Dabney. *Secrets of the Great City*. Jones Brothers & Co., 1868. https://archive.org/details/secretsofgreatcio1mcca.

Mikorenda, Jerry. *Elizabeth Jennings, Chester A. Arthur, and the Early Fight for Civil Rights*. Lyons, 2020.

New York (State) and Montgomery H. (Montgomery Hunt) Throop. *The Revised Statutes of the States of New York: As Altered by Subsequent Legislation: Together with the Other Statutory Provisions of a General and Permanent Nature Now in Force, Passed from the Year 1778 to the Close of the Session of the Legislature of 1881*. 7th ed. Banks & Brothers, 1882.

Northup, Solomon. *Twelve Years a Slave*. 1853; Digireads.com, 2009.

Paine, Albert Bigelow. *Thomas Nast. His Period and His Pictures*. Macmillan, 1904.

Parton, Ethel. *The Lost Locket: The Newburyport of 1830*. Viking, 1940.

———. *Melissa Ann*. Penguin, 1955.

———. *Penelope Ellen*. Bethlehem, 2015.

———. *Tabitha Mary: A Little Girl of 1810*. Viking, 1935.

———. *Vinny Applegay: A Story of the 1870s*. Viking, 1937.

Parton, James, with Horce Greeley, T. W. Higginson, J. S. C. Abbott, James M. Hoppin, William Winter, Theodore Tilton, Fanny Fern, Grace Greenwood, and E. C. Stanton. *Eminent Women of the Age: Being Narratives of the Lives and Deeds of the Most Prominent Women of the Present Generation*. 1869; HardPress, 2018.

Penny, Virginia. *Employments of Women*. D. E. Fisk and Co., 1870.

Perkins, Maureen. *Visions of the Future: Almanacs, Times, and Cultural Changes*. Oxford University Press, 2005.

Peterson, Carla L. *Black Gotham: A Family History of African Americans in Nineteenth-Century New York City*. Yale University Press, 2011.

Ptacin, Mira. *The In-Betweens: The Spiritualists, Mediums, and Legends of Camp Etna*. Liveright, 2019.

Quinlan, Heather E. *Plagues, Pandemics, and Viruses: From the Plague of Athens to COVID-19*. Visible Ink, 2020.

Richmond, Rev. J. F. *New York and Its Institutions 1609–1873*. E. B. Treat, 1872.

Riis, Jacob A. *How the Other Half Lives: Studies Among the Tenements of New York*. Penguin, 1997.

Robinson, Solon. *Hot Corn: Life Scenes in New York Illustrated*. DeWitt and Davenport, 1854.

Sanger, William. *The History of Prostitution: Its Extent, Causes, Effects throughout the World*. 1858; Anboco, 2016.

Schmidgall, Gary, ed. *Conserving Walt Whitman's Fame*. Iowa University Press, 2006.

Seitz, Sharon, and Stuart Miller. *The Other Islands of New York City: A History and Guide*. Countryman, 2011.

Seraile, William. *Angels of Mercy: White Women and the History of New York's Colored Orphan Asylum*. Empire State Editions, 2013.

Silver-Isenstadt, Jean L. *Shameless: The Visionary Life of Mary Gove Nichols*. Johns Hopkins University Press, 2002.

Slater, Fletcher Daniel. "The Life and Letters of Mortimer Thomson." Master's thesis, Northwestern University, 1931. https://www.undercover.hosting.nyu.edu/s/undercover-reporting/item/14060.

Stansell, Christine. *City of Women: Sex and Class in New York 1789–1860*. University of Illinois Press, 1987.

Stiles, Henry R. *A History of the City of Brooklyn: The Old Town and Village of Brooklyn, the Town of Bushwick, the Village and City of Williamsburgh*. 1870; HardPress, 2018.

Strong, George Templeton. *The Diary of George Templeton Strong: The Turbulent Fifties, 1850–1859*. Macmillan, 1952.

Thomas, Keith. *Religion and the Decline of Magic: Studies in Popular Beliefs in Sixteenth- and Seventeenth-Century England*. 1971; Penguin, 1991.

Turner, Hy B. *When Giants Ruled: The Story of Park Row, New York's Great Newspaper Street*. Fordham University Press, 1999.

Van Cleve, Charlotte Ouisconsin. *"Three Score Years and Ten": Life-Long Memories of Fort Snelling, Minnesota, and Other Parts of the West*. 1888; e-book ed., 2011.

Walling, George Washington. *Recollections of a New York Chief of Police*. Caxton Concern Limited, 1887.

Warren, Joyce W. *Fanny Fern: An Independent Woman*. Rutgers University Press, 1992.

Weisberg, Barbara. *Talking to the Dead: Kate and Maggie Fox and the Rise of Spiritualism*. HarperSanFrancisco, 2005.

Wells, Jonathan Daniel. *The Kidnapping Club: Wall Street, Slavery, and Resistance on the Eve of the Civil War*. Hachette, 2020.

Whitman, Walt. *Walt Whitman's Selected Journalism*. University of Iowa Press, 2015.

Willrich, Michael. *Pox: An American History*. Penguin, 2011.

Ziegelman, Jane. *97 Orchard: An Edible History of Five Immigrant Families in One New York Tenement*. HarperCollins, 2010.

INDEX

and, 112; 1850s, 6–7; male writers on,
7–8
stagecoaches, 44
Stansell, Christine, 2, 48
Star Tribune, 103
State Emigrant Refuge, 108
Stille, Helen C., 23
Stiner, W. H., 116
Stockton, Frank, 136
storytelling, Tarot element of, 5
Stowe, Harriet Beecher, 31, 57
Street, Francis Scott, 101
Strong, George Templeton, 10, 122
Stuyvesant, John R., 120–22
Stuyvesant, Peter, 100, 120
suffragette movement, 42, 101, 137
suicide: potion and place for committing,
48; Stein sisters, 20
Swedenborg, Emanuel, 6

Tammany Hall, 29
Tarot decks, 23; Lenormand, 8, 25, 115;
playing cards as, 70–71; Rider-Waite-
Smith, 4–5; Shakespearean, 4
Tarot readings: first, 4; storytelling element
of, 5; therapeutic nature of, 5
tenant-houses, 54, 112
Ten Broek slave sale, 71–76
Ten Days in a Mad-House (Bly), 107
tenements, 48–49, 53, 89, 109
Tennyson, Lord Alfred, 30
Thomson, Clifford, 87, 100, 102, 114; on
Parton, J., and Eldredge, E., 135; son's
drowning, 136
Thomson, Mark (son of Thomson, M.), 62,
90, 118, 132; death of, 136
Thomson, Mortimer Neal (Doesticks): acts
of heroism, 76–77, 87, 100; alcoholism
of, 108; biography on, 7; cirrhosis of
liver, 108; Civil War roles of, 85; critics
of, 15–16; Dana's discovery of, 15;
death of, 105, 108, 114, 133–34; death
of father, 102; debate over authorship
and, 119; downward spiral of, 99, 104;
drinking of Eytinge, S., and, 32; as
editor of *Star Tribune*, 103; 1866 series
of Doesticks letters, 100–101; Eldredge,

G., courtship, 57, 60–61; Eytinge,
S., and, 31–32; father of, 89–90, 102;
female disguise of, 9–10, 12; first book
of, 15, 17; funeral service for, 115–17;
habit of losing things, 86–87; hoax on
death of, 16; inaccuracies of Doesticks
and, 3; Inebriate Asylum and, 105–7,
108; intoxication while in Twenty-Sixth
regiment, 85; as IRS storekeeper, 103;
jewelry store clerk job of, 13–14, 34;
last writings of, 100; lecture circuit of,
29–30; as living with brother and family,
102; marriage to Eldredge, G., 61–63;
marriage to Van Cleve, A., 42, 43;
mockery and patriarchy of, 7; mother
of, 89, 114–15; narration style, "Cash
Customer" and, 2; Nast and, 29–30;
newspapers publishing articles by, 15;
obituary, 14, 118; original manuscript
of, 2–3; other writers compared with,
6; parents and brother, 12; popularity
decline of, 100; pranks in war, 85–86;
Prince of Wales and, 28; pseudonym
(Doesticks) of, 2; pulp fiction writing
of, 101; reception of work by, 15–17;
rise to fame, 14; similarity with women
mocked by, 111; slave sale attended by,
71–76; smallpox contracted by, 42–43;
son of, 62; spiritualists mocked by, 7;
study of medicine, 102; suffragettes criticized by, 101–2; tombstone and burial,
117–18; in traveling theater troupe, 13;
Tribune articles of, 2, 7–8, 10; tricks of,
13; university expulsion of, 13; Wells
and, 13, 14; wife's money spent by,
90–91; works of, 17; writing career start
of, 14; as young boy, 12–13. *See also*
Doesticks, Q. K. Philander, P.B.; *specific
fortune tellers*; *specific topics*
Thomson, Sophia Edna (mother of Thomson, Mortimer): death of, 118; poem
written by, 114–15; pseudonym of, 114
Tiernay, Bridget, 37
Tilton, Elizabeth, 118
tintypes, 90
Tombs, the, 83, 92
tonics, 51

Marie Carter is a Scottish-born writer, tour guide, and tour guide developer who has been based in New York City for the last twenty-three years. Fascinated by New York City's macabre and little-known histories in her writing and life, she is a licensed tour guide, as well as researcher and developer with Boroughs of the Dead, a walking tour company that specializes in strange, macabre, and ghostly walking tours of New York City. Marie leads tours in Astoria, Roosevelt Island, Manhattan, and Brooklyn. She is also a frequent guest lecturer at QED Astoria. Her first book, based on her experiences in learning trapeze, *The Trapeze Diaries*, was published by Hanging Loose Press. Her novel *Holly's Hurricane* was published in 2018 and was a finalist for the 2019 Montaigne Medal. She was also the editor of *Word Jig: New Fiction from Scotland* (Hanging Loose Press). She has been a guest speaker on NPR's *Ask Me Another*, BBC Radio Lincolnshire, *The Expat Chit Chat Show*, and *Talking Hart Island*, and she has been written about or featured in the *New York Times*, *Huffington Post*, *QNS*, *Queens Gazette*, and many other media outlets. She has made an appearance on PIX11. Her work has been published in *The Best of Creative Nonfiction* (Norton) and *Nineteenth Century Magazine*, a publication of the Victorian Society in America.